고은—**나의 파도소리**

The Sound of My Waves

답게
한국문학 영역총서

이 책은 Cornell East Asia Series No. 68로 1993년에 미국 코넬대학에서 간행된 바 있는
*The Sound of My Waves*의 한국어 대역판으로, Cornell East Asia Series와 공동출판의
형식으로 나온 것임을 밝힌다.

번역판권 ⓒ 안토니 / 김영무
원작판권 ⓒ 고 은

펴낸이 / 一庚 장소님
옮긴이 / 안토니, 김영무
지은이 / 고 은
펴낸곳 / 도서 **답게**

초판인쇄일 / 1996년 11월 10일
초판발행일 / 1996년 11월 15일
주소 / 137-064 서울 서초구 방배4동 829-22호 원빌딩 201호
등록 / 1990년 2월 28일, 제21-140호
전화 / 편집 591-8267, 영업 537-0464, 596-0464
팩시밀리 / 594-0464
ISBN 89-7574-070-6

This bilingual edition is a joint publication with the Cornell University East Asia
Program. An English language only edition was originally published in 1993 under the
same title as number 68 in the Cornell East Asia Series (ISSN 1050-2955), Cornell
University East Asia Program, 140 Uris Hall, Ithaca, NY 14853-7601, ISBN
0-939657-87-2 cloth, ISBN 0-939657-68-6 paper.

Original Poems ⓒ Ko Un
Translation ⓒ 1996 Brother Anthony and Young-Moo Kim

Published by DapGae Books
#201 Won Bld
829-22 Bangbae 4-dong, Socho-ku, Seoul 137-064 Korea
Tel/(02)591-8267, 537-0464, 596-0464 Fax/594-0464

Cornell East Asia Program
Cornell University
Ithaca, New York 14853

Printed and bound in the Republic of Korea

No. 68, Cornell East Asia Series ISSN 1050-2955
Cornell East Asia Program ISBN 1-885445-72-5
값 7,000원

DapGae
English Translations
of Korean Literature Series

Editor : Young-Moo Kim

고은—나의 파도소리

The Sound of My Waves

Selected Poems by *Ko Un*

Translated by Brother Anthony of Taizé / Young-Moo Kim

돌샘 답게

머리말

파란만장이라는 한자의 표현이 있다. 변화가 많은 삶, 태산같은 파도에 시달려온 삶, 요컨대 순탄하지 않은 삶을 말할 때 우리는 이런 표현을 쓴다. 이 시집의 제목에서 우리가 그 소리를 듣도록 초대되고 있는 태산 같은 파도의 삶을 살아온 시인이 바로 고은 시인이다.

추위로 사람이 얼어죽기도 하지만
사람이 추위에 깊어집니다

는 그의 시구절 그대로 그는 고통과 힘 사이의 관계가 어떤 것인지를 탐색할 기회를 많이 가졌던 시인이다.

일본 식민지 치하였던 1933년 전라북도 군산에서 태어난 고은은 매우 조숙해서, 만 여덟 살 때 벌써 머리 큰 소년들도 어려움을 겪는 한문 공부를 상당한 수준까지 했다. 소학교 3학년 때는 수신 시간에 장래의 희망을 묻는 일본인 교장에게 천황폐하가 되겠다고 했다가 천황모독죄로 심한 벌을 받았다. 열두 살이 되던 1945년 학교가 끝나고 집으로 가던 길에 우연히 문둥이 시인 한하운의 『한하운 시초』를 길가에서 주어 밤새도록 읽고 "가슴이 찢어질 것 같은 문학적 충격"을 받기도 했다. 1950년 6월 한국전쟁이 터지던 해, 그는 인민군에게 끌려가 폭격으로 파손된 비행장 활주로를 고치는 일에 강제동원 되기도 했고, 형제가 형제를 죽이는 싸움에 소년

적, 전원적 순결이 산산이 부서지는 체험을 하면서, 정신착란상태를 헤매기도 했으며, 자살을 시도하기도 했다.

동란이 끝나기 전인 1952년 불교승려가 되어 효봉스님의 상좌가 된 이래 그는 10년 동안 참선과 방랑생활을 하며 구걸행각을 했다. 1957년에는 다른 스님과 함께 《불교신문》을 창간, 초대 주필이 되어 많은 논설과 시를 발표하던 중, 1958년 작품 「폐결핵」이 당시의 유명한 시인 조지훈의 추천으로 《현대시》에 발표됨으로써 문단에 데뷔했고(한국에서는 유명시인의 추천을 받아야 정식으로 문단에 나온다), 1960년 처녀시집 『피안감성』이 출간되었다.

불교 승려가 된 이래, 전등사 주지, 해인사 교무 및 주지 대리, 전국승려대회 지도위원 등 불교계에서도 이름을 날리던 고은은, 1962년 《한국일보》에 놀랍게도 환속선언문을 발표함과 동시에, 십 년간의 승려생활을 청산하고 불교계를 떠난다. 이 무렵 러시아 소설가 숄로호프의 『조용한 돈강』을 일본어 번역으로 읽고 그 장대함에 충격을 받아 그 동안 써둔 원고를 불질러 버리고 절망에 빠지기도 했다. 1963년부터 제주도에 머물면서 자선 학교를 차려 교장 겸 국어 미술 교사로 무료 수업을 했고, 두 번째 시집 『해변의 운문집』을 출간했다. 1967년 다시 서울로 올라온 이래, 폭음과 자학의 생활을 하며 시, 소설, 수필 등 많은 글을 썼고, 1970년에 다시 약을 먹고 자살을 기도하여 의식불명의 상태에서 서른 시간만에 깨어나기도 했다.

1973년은 시인의 삶에 하나의 커다란 변화가 일어난 시기로써, 이 때부터 이른바 허무주의의 대표자라는 명성을 버리고, 사회·역사적 사건에 직접적으로 참여하는 전투적인 민족 시인으로 탈바꿈을 하게 된다. 박정희

대통령의 삼선개헌 반대운동에 뛰어든 이래로 그 동안 수많은 민권운동에 적극적으로 참여하면서, 자유실천문인협의회를 구성하여 초대 대표간사가 되며, 수시로 경찰과 정보부에 잡혀갔으며, 여러 차례 감옥생활도 경험했다. 이와 같이 한국민주화운동의 핵심적 지도인물의 하나로 눈부신 활약을 하는 중에도 『문의 마을에 가서』(1974), 『입산』(1977), 『새벽길』(1978), 『조국의 별』(1984) 등 빼어난 시집과 『당시선(唐詩選)』 및 『두보시선(杜甫詩選)』 등 번역시집을 비롯해서 유명시인들의 전기 등 많은 책을 출간했다.

1983년 고은 시인의 일생에서 또 한번의 변화가 일어난다. 첫 시집 『피안감성』이 나온 1960년 이후 20여년 간의 세월에 걸쳐 출간된 여섯 일곱 권의 시집과 기타 장시들을 한데 묶은 『고은 시전집』이 이 해에 나왔다. 그 동안 남다른 옹이와 뒤틀림이 유난히 많았던 지난 25년간의 시작활동을 일단 총정리하는 일이 긴요했던 모양이다. 그의 삶은 다시 한번 완전히 새로운 행로를 밟게 되는데, 물론 이 시기는 시인 자신이 목숨의 위협을 받았던 1980년 5월의 광주 학살 직후 때이기도 하다.

오십 평생 독신을 고수하던 그가 1983년 5월 젊은 영문학교수와 결혼을 하여 서울에서 자동차로 2시간 가량 걸리는 안성으로 이사를 했고, 일 년 뒤에는 딸아이도 태어나는 등 떠돌이 승려였던 이 시인에게 가정이 생기게 되었다. 그리고 안성 시대의 개막과 더불어 그의 창조활동도 전에 없이 활발하여, 안성으로 이주한 지 10년 가량 되는 최근까지 『전원시편』(1986), 『시여, 날아가라』(1986), 『네 눈동자』(1988), 『아침 이슬』(1990), 『눈물을 위하여』(1991), 『해금강』(1991), 『만인보』1-9권, 서사시 『백두산』의 첫 두 권 등의 출간을 보게 된다. 이것은 총 900 페이지를 가득 채워 두 권으로 간행된 전집의 분량을 훨씬 상회하는 것이고, 『만인보』와 『백두산』은 지금까지 보다 더 많은 분량이 기약되어 곧 속간될 예정이다.

이와 같이 고은 시인의 시는 기왕에 나온 것만도 분량이 엄청나게 많고, 더구나 지금 이 시점이야말로 그의 창조력의 밀물이 한창 용솟음치고 있는 때인 만큼, 그의 시세계를 한 마디로 뭐라고 규정하기는 불가능한 일처럼 보인다. 이런 한계를 분명히 인정하면서, 고은의 시세계를 잠시 살펴보기로 하겠다.

우선 자명한 것부터 짚고 넘어가자. 그는 우리 나라의 그 어느 시인보다 많은 작품을 썼고, 그가 쓴 시의 종류도 두서너 줄의 짧은 단상시(斷想詩)로부터, 짧게는 수십 행 길게는 수백 행에 걸치는 장시, 서사시, 전원시, 또 무엇보다도 그가 창조한 새로운 형식의 역사시라고 할 수 있는 『만인보』의 시편에 이르기까지 매우 다양하다. 그는 예민한 감수성, 뛰어난 직관력, 상상력의 깊이와 넓이, 언어사용의 능수 능란함, 삶에 대한 성숙한 이해력 등을 두루 갖춘 한국 시문학사상 최초의 큰 시인(Major poet)인 것이다.

처녀 시집 『피안감성』(1960)에서 『해변의 운문집』(1966)과 『신, 언어 최후의 마을』(1967)에 이르는 시기의 시들은 주로 삶의 허무함과 무상함을 탐미적 감각으로 형상화한 것들이다.

그 뒤 1970년대 중반에 나온 『문의 마을에 가서』(1974) 이후 고은의 시에는 새로운 역사의식이 담기기 시작하면서, 70년대 후반의 『입산』 및 『입산 이후』를 거쳐 『새벽길』(1979)에 이르면 매우 전투적인 정치적 감각의 시들이 그의 시의 주류를 이룬다.

안성으로 집을 옮긴 후 처음 발간된 『전원시편』, 특히 1984년 중반에 나온 『조국의 별』에서 고은의 시는 또 한번의 변모를 보여준다. 이 변모의 뒷면에는 광주의 오월과 관계된 투옥 및 죽음의 체험이 작용한다. 그는 육군교도소 특수 감방에 수용되어 언제 죽을지 모르는 나날을 보내기도 했다.

암흑의 감방에서 절망하지 않고 살아남아 있으면서, 시인은 하나의 목숨이 태어나 성장하는데는 엄청난 시간과 노력과 보살핌이 소요되는데, 그런 목숨을 죽여 없애기는 또한 얼마나 쉬운가, 사람의 목숨이라는 것이 얼마나 사라지기 쉬운 것인가 하는 목숨의 순간성을 새삼 절감한다. 물론 그는 전에도 목숨의 순간성과 찰나성을 모르지 않았다. 그것을 너무나 잘 알았기에 그는 그 허무함에 절망하여 몇 번이나 자살을 꾀했고, 삶의 허무한 순간성에 대한 예민한 인식은 고은 시의 출발의 한 주요 동력이었다. 그러나 삼라만상의 삶이 순간적이요 찰나적이라는 사실 앞에서 허무감과 무상함을 느끼고 절망했던 지난날과는 달리, 시시각각 목숨의 위협을 구체적으로 겪어 가는 육군형무소 송장 넣는 관 같은 특감의 절박한 상황에서 시인은 오히려 그 짧은 목숨이 바로 그 순간성과 찰나성으로 하여 정녕 얼마나 고귀하고 숭엄한 것인가를 깨닫는다.

이제 고은이 시인으로서 스스로 다짐하며 떠안은 사명은 이런 고귀한 목숨을, 그것이 아무리 지지리 못나고, 찌들고, 별볼일 없고, 심지어 고약한 인생의 것이라 해도, 망각으로 영영 사라져 없어지지 않게 되살리는 일이었다. 그는 자신이 이 세상에 태어나 알게 된 모든 사람들에 대해 노래하기로 마음먹게 되며, 그 결심의 첫 열매가 아직도 진행중인 『만인보』의 창조작업이다. 이 노래들에서 우리는 수많은 인물과 사건을 목도하게 되는

9

데, 우리 역사의 날줄과 씨줄을 이루는 민중의 삶의 맥박 자체를, 우리들 삶의 호흡 자체를 하나의 배경으로서가 아니라, 살아 뜀뛰는 그 모습 그대로 만나게 된다.

『만인보』의 시편들은 고급한 언어예술인 시와는 무관한 것으로 푸대접을 받아온 이른바 투박한 민중언어의 무한한 예술적 가능성을 극적으로 확인시켜주고 있다. 물론 이런 노력은 과거에도 있어 왔고 1970년대 이후 신경림의 빼어난 업적을 비롯해서 많은 젊은 시인들의 손에서 이런 노력은 성실히 계속되고 있다. 그리고 급기야는 노동현장의 체험을 직접 육성으로 들려주는 훌륭한 노동시도 또한 씌어지고 있다. 그러나 『만인보』에서 처럼 민중언어와 민중적 삶 사이에 한 치의 틈도 없는 시적 성취는 찾아보기 힘들었다.

그리고 이러한 시들은 의식적으로 예술적이려는 안달의 언어가 아니라, 더없이 넉넉하고 수다스러우면서도 흐트러짐이 없고, 유연하면서도 뻣뻣하고, 싱싱하게 살아오는 민중언어로 이루어지고 있어서 더욱 감동적이다.

『만인보』와 『백두산』 서사시의 창조작업과 병행하여 고은의 시는 지금도 계속 쏟아져 나오고 있다. 1990년 말에 나온 시집 『눈물을 위하여』의 뒷글에서 시인은 "역사적이기 위해서 역사를 타파"하고, "현실과 우주를 한꺼번에 획득"하기 위해 자신이 죽은 뒤 "무덤까지도" 시가 되지 않으면 안되겠지만, 그러나 "나는 시 자체로부터 언제나 해방되어 있다"고 적고 있다.

또 1991년 4월에 나온 시집 『해금강』의 저자의 말에서도 시 창작의 의미에 관해, "내가 죽은 뒤 몇 년 뒤 누군가가 내 무덤을 파헤쳐본다면 거기에도 내 뼈 대신 내가 무덤의 어둠 속에서 쓴 시로 꽉 차 있을 것이다

······내가 너무 시에 집착하나? 하기야 시와의 결별 바로 옆에서 내 시는 실재하기 때문에 내 집착은 시로부터의 해탈에 속한다"고 말하고 있거니와, 이 시인의 다양하고 분방한 시세계를 한 마디로 요약할 수 있는 낱말을 굳이 찾자면 "해방"이라는 낱말을 들 수밖에 없을 것 같다. 그는 이 낱말이 뜻하는 모든 의미에서 해방의 시인이다. 자신의 모든 삶이 아니 죽은 뒤의 무덤까지도 시여야 한다고 고집하면서도, 시 자체로부터는 후련히 해방되어 있는 시인, 그것이 고은 시인이다.

Introduction

by Young-Moo Kim

There is a traditional Korean expression that speaks of "waves ten thousand feet high." It is used to refer to someone who has experienced dramatic "ups and downs," who has been through immense difficulties in the course of what was, in short, the very opposite of a "quiet life." The life of the poet Ko Un offers a prime example of ten-thousand-foot high waves: those waves, perhaps, that we are invited to listen to in the title of this volume. Ko Un has had ample opportunity to explore the link between suffering and strength. As he himself once wrote:

> People freeze to death in the cold, of course,
> but people also grow deeper by the cold

Born in 1933 in the city of Kunsan in Korea's North Cholla Province, when Korea was under Japanese rule, he was an extremely precocious child. By the time he was eight, he had already studied classical Chinese texts that even much older children usually had difficulty in mastering. When he was in grade three, his Japanese headmaster asked him what he hoped to become in the future and got the answer, "The Emperor of Japan." Ko Un was severely punished for this effrontery. One day in 1945, when he was twelve, on his way home from school he picked up a book of poems lying by the wayside. It was the well-known leper-poet

Han Ha-Un's *Selected Poems*. He stayed up all night reading it. He describes his reaction: "My breast seemed torn apart by the force of the shock those lyrics produced on me." In June 1950, when the Korean War broke out, he was forcibly mobilized by the People's Army to repair the bomb- damaged runways of an air-force base, and the experience of fratricidal warfare effectively destroyed his rural childhood innocence, bringing him to the verge of mental breakdown, and to attempted suicide.

Before the war was over, in 1952, he joined the Buddhist clergy and became the recognized disciple of the great monk Hyo Bong. For the next ten years he lived a life of Zen meditation, always on the move. He travelled the whole country living by alms. In 1957 he and another monk founded the Buddhist Newspaper. As its first editor-in-chief, he began to publish essays and poems. In 1958 he made his formal debut in the literary world, when his short poem "Tuberculosis" was published in the review Modern Poetry at the recommendation of the renowned poet Cho Chi-hun; for in the Korean literary world you are not recognized as a real poet unless your poems are commended by some renowned writer. Ko Un's first collection of youthful poems, *Other World Sensitivity,* was published in 1960.

By this time Ko Un had become quite well known in Buddhist circles. He was head priest of Chondung Temple, then education director and acting head of Haein Temple, and finally a member of the Central Committee of the National Monks' Association. Many people were astonished when he published a Resignation Manifesto in the *Hankook Daily News* and left the Buddhist community in 1962. At this time he read Mikhail Sholokov's *Quiet Flows the Don* in a Japanese translation, and according to Ko Un, this great Russian novel caused such a great shock by its sheer magnitude and complexity, that he burnt his accumulated manuscripts and fell into despair. From 1963 until 1967 he lived on the southern island of Cheju, managing a charity school where he was simultaneously headmaster, teacher of Korean and of art, working without pay. At this time he published his second volume of poems, *Seaside Poems*. When he returned to Seoul in 1967, he began a period marked by heavy drinking and self-torment, during which he wrote many poems, as well as novels and essays, until another suicide attempt in 1970. He was in a coma for thirty hours after taking poison before regaining consciousness in hospital.

In 1973 another great change occurred in Ko Un's career. Rejecting his reputation as a spokesman of Nihilism, he became a militant nationalist poet, actively involved in contemporary social and political events. He took a leading role in the drive against president Park Chung-hee's plan to amend the Constitution to allow himself a third term in office. Ko Un continues to be actively involved in the seemingly endless Korean struggle for human rights, and when the Association of Artists for Practical Freedom was established, he became its first secretary-general. He has been arrested many times and served several prison terms. Despite all this intense activity as a key figure of the Korean democracy movements, he has written and published prolifically: his books include collections of poems (*On the Way to Munui Village* (1974), *Going into Mountain Seclusion* (1977), *Early Morning Road* (1978), *Homeland Stars* (1984)), translations from the Chinese (*Selected Poems of the Tang Dynasty* and *Selected Poems of Tu Fu*), biographies of famous poets and other works.

In 1983 the poet's life seemed to take yet another turn with the publication of *Ko Un's Collected Poems* containing the poems published in his six or seven volumes since 1960, as well as other, previously uncollected poems first published separately. It had apparently become urgent for him to bring some kind of order into the poetic activities of the past twenty-five years, years that had been characterized by a remarkable series of dramatic ups and downs, of ten-thousand-foot waves. Once again, his life took on a completely new shape as he embarked on a new course, just a few years after the traumatic Kwangju Massacre of May 1980, when his own life had been threatened.

After 50 years of solitary life, in May 1983 Ko Un married a younger woman, a professor of English Literature, and they went to live in the countryside at Ansong, about two hours' drive from Seoul. A year later, a daughter was born, the former monk had a family. Since the move to Ansong, Ko Un's creative powers have entered a phase of unparalleled productivity; in recent years numerous new volumes of poems have appeared, including *Pastoral Poems* (1986), *Fly High, Poem!* (1986), *Your Eyes* (1988), *Morning Dew* (1990), *For Tears* (1991), *Sea Diamond Mountain* (1991), the nine volumes of *Ten Thousand Lives,* and the four volumes containing the first two books of the epic *Paektu Mountain.* In just five years, far more than the nine hundred or so pages of the 1983 *Collected Poems* have appeared, and major new portions of both *Ten Thousand Lives* and *Paektu Mountain* are in preparation.

With the vast amount of work already produced, and with his creative powers just now reaching their height, the essential features of Ko Un's poetry can hardly be captured in a few pages. All we can do is describe briefly a few of the main characteristics of his work.

To begin with the obvious: Ko Un has written far more than any other Korean poet, and manifested an immense diversity: epigrams of a couple of lines, poems with dozens of lines, or hundreds of lines; long discursive poems; epic; pastoral; and even a genre of poem he has himself created, which we may term the popular-historical poem, in *Ten Thousand Lives*. For his keen sensitivity, outstanding powers of intuition, the breadth and depth of his imagination and his skillful use of language, as well as the maturity of his understanding of human life, Ko Un is widely acknowledged to be Korea's foremost contemporary poet.

Most of the poems of the earliest period, from the youthful poems of *Other World Sensitivity* (1960) until those in *Seaside Poems* (1966) and *Village of Gods and Words* (1967), strive to represent the futile and transitory nature of life, and are marked by a strongly aestheticizing sensitivity.

From the mid-seventies, with the collection *On the way to Munui Village* (1974), Ko Un's poems begin to be marked by a historical approach, while the volumes published in the later seventies, *Going into Mountain Seclusion, After Mountain Seclusion* (1977), and *Early Morning Road* (1978) are characterized by a highly militant, more clearly political tone.

The poems written after the move to Ansong, the *Pastoral Poems* and in particular the *Homeland Stars* of the mid-80s, show yet another transformation in Ko Un's poetics. Underlying it are the effects of the events connected with the Kwangju Uprising of May 1980, when hundreds of citizens were killed by Korean army troops, the poet's imprisonment and his confrontation with death. Confined in a special section of a military prison, he did not know from one day to the next if he was going to be executed or not.

Bravely clinging to life in a narrow cell, the poet acutely sensed life's fragility: how for one single life to be born and develop demands long years, great efforts, intense care, and yet how easy it is for that life to be crushed and extinguished. Needless to say, this sense of life's impermanence was not unknown to Ko Un before this. His sense of life's futility had been acute enough to provoke those attempts at suicide; and indeed a strong sense of life's emptiness and impermanence is one of the major impulses underlying Ko Un's entire career as a poet. But in contrast to the despair of earlier days, when his response to the impermanence of life had been nihilism and instability, from his confrontation in the coffin-like cell of a military prison with the fact that his life might end at any moment, the poet came to a realization that life is precious and sublime precisely because of its impermanence.

This helps to explain why Ko Un has given himself the mission to preserve in poetry a huge number of precious human lives, no matter how uncommendable, weary, commonplace, or wicked, preventing them from sliding forever into oblivion. He has resolved to represent in poems every person he has ever encountered since he was born into the world, and the result is the creation of the poems of his *Ten Thousand Lives,* which is still in progress. In these poems we encounter a host of characters and incidents, finding ourselves face-to-face with the very pulse-beat of ordinary Korean people's daily life, all that has gone to make up the map we call our nation's recent history, not as some kind of background, but as itself, leaping alive in each poem.

Ten Thousand Lives offers dramatic proof of the artistic potential latent in the language of the common people, a language that has hitherto been shunned as unworthy of the sophisticated, refined verbal pyrotechnics deemed proper to poetry. This is not an entirely new enterprise; in contemporary Korean poetry many poets have been striving with great ardour in this direction, beginning with the outstanding achievements of Shin Kyongnim in the early 1970s. Most recently, magnificent "workers' poems" have been published that give a direct expression to experience in the work-place. But it would be hard to find a poetic achievement equal to *Ten Thousand Lives* with its perfect blend of popular language and the lives portrayed.

These poems are not written in a nervously self-conscious language. They are all the more effective for being in a popular language that is copious, loquacious yet not untidy, calm but crisp, and vividly expressive.

Together with his on-going work on *Ten Thousand Lives* and the vast epic *Paektu Mountain,* Ko Un continues to pour out other poems. In the epilogue to one of his most recent volumes, *For Tears,* published in late 1990, he writes: "in order to be historical, I overthrow history" and "in order to gain possession of present and cosmos, I must continue to become a poem even after death, in the tomb." At the same time, he insists, "I am constantly liberating myself from the poem as such."

The poet's sense of this process of poetic creation is stated even more clearly in the foreword to the collection *Sea Diamond Mountain,* published in April 1991: "If someone opens my grave a few years after my death, they will find it full, not of my bones, but of poems written in that tomb's darkness······ Am I too attached to poetry? Because my poems exist side-by-side with a farewell to poetry, my attachment is one aspect of a deliverance from poetry." If we are looking for one word to characterize the poet's multifarious and unrestrained poetic activities, the only possible word is "liberation." He is a poet of liberation, in every sense of the word. He wants to make his entire life, and even his grave, a poem, while refusing to let himself be imprisoned by the effort to write poetry as an end in itself.

차   례
Contents

신, 언어 최후의 마을(1967)
Village of Gods and Words

2

문의 마을에 가서(1974)
On the Way to Munui Village

입산(1977)
Going into Mountain Seclusion

입산 이후(1977)
After Mountain Seclusion

새벽길(1978)
Early Morning Road

3

조국의 별(1984)
Homeland Stars

전원시편(1986)
Pastoral Poems

시여, 날아가라(1986)
Fly High, Poem!

네 눈동자(1988)
Your Eyes

아침이슬(1990)
Morning Dew

눈물을 위하여(1990)
For Tears

4

만인보(1986〜)
Ten Thousand Lives

1

천은사 운(韻)

그이들끼리
살데.

골짜구니 아래도 그 위에도
그이들의 얼얼이 떠서
바람으로 들리데.

그이들은
밤 솔바람소리.

바위 보아
비인 산허리.

가을이 오데.

바위를 골라
나앉아 우는 추녀 끝
뜰에 떨어지는 풍경소리에

그이들끼리
살데.

Chon-un Temple

They live
in a world of their own

Their spirits go floating
under the cliffs and high above,
they are the wind echoing

a night sound
of wind in pine trees.

Rocks rest
on bare mountain slopes.

Now autumn is coming.

They hear wind-bell chimes
drop to the temple courtyards
from the eaves perched
weeping on rocks.

They live
in a world of their own.

돌아가 한 번 잊은 제
도로 가고 싶은
그이들의 얼 바람진 산허리

그이들은
살데.

그이들은
살데.

All left all forgotten
now comes a wish to return
to the mountain slopes
swept by their floating spirits

where
they
live

they
live.

밤의 법열(法悅)

아 어머니는 아니 주무실 테고
밤으로
밤낮으로
흐르는 것 다 고요가 되니
가으내 간 그 물소리 어느 만큼 가 자는지
아 춥고 기꺼워라. 이러하다가
어느덧 나의 몸으로부터 나아 가는 물소리로
어두움아 나의 마음을 비치어 보아라.

Night Ecstasy

Asleep, Mother? Surely not asleep?
All the things that flow
by day, by night, are silent now.
How far, I wonder, has the water's murmur gone
to take its sleep, that I heard all autumn long?
Cold, yes, but full of joy.
Very soon, deep dark, you'll see my heart
reflected in the water's murmur
surging up within me.

봄 비

물결이여 네가 잠든 물 우의 고요에
봄비는 내려와 죽는다.
물 우에 물 속의 어둠이 솟아올라도
물결이여
네가 잠든 물 우에 받는 봄비로
먼데까지도 봄비로
먼데 바위까지도 봄이게 한다.
아 너와 내가 잠든 물 우의 여기에도
한 덩어리 바위가 침묵으로 떠오르는다.
허나 봄비는 내려와 죽는다.

Spring rain

On your sleeping silence, wave,
spring rain falls and dies.
The night dark in the water may soar up
but by the spring rain on your sleeping water
wave
far away by that rain's power
far away rocks are turned to spring.
Above this water where we two lie sleeping
a rocky mass looms, all silence.
But still the spring rain falls and dies.

잠

내가 아무리 잠자도
달밤은 휘영청
그대로이리

문득 잠 깨어
돌아누으면……

눈감으면
이미 들어온 달빛이야
내 몸이 되리

서산마루에
지는 달 받을 만치
다 구름을 씻어 놓았느뇨

달밤에 그림자 이루듯이
내 잠도 이제 잠그림자이리

Sleep

No matter how deeply I sleep
the moonlit night
remains as bright as ever.

If I wake with a start
turn
and nestle down again

once my eyes have closed
the moonlight trapped inside them
becomes part of me.

But are the clouds washed pure?
Pure enough for the moon
as it drops behind the western hills?

Now my sleep is a shadow of sleep,
a shadow cast on a moonlit night.

벌레소리

늦가을 잎 다 지고
아조 나무가지들 비어 있을 때
그때야말로
땅 밑으로 어두운 물줄기는 흐르는가
땅 밑 물줄기가 어쩌다 솟아오르듯
그런 솟아오르는 물소리가
내 꿈 깨이자 들리더니
그 소리는 어디로 돌아가고
푸른 밤중에 다시 잠 이루려 할 때
나는 내 귀가 아니라
내 눈으로 듣나니
내 눈의 벌레소리 외마디 깊음이여
귀 없다
소리 없다
눈의 어둠으로 깨친 새벽이여

Insect buzz

The leaves are all down,
the branches are stretching bare;
is a dark stream flowing underground
in such a season?
A rushing sound startles me out of a dream,
like water somehow gushing underground;
it fades away, then deep in the blue night
as I try to get back to sleep, I hear it again,
not with my ears
but with my eyes.
My eyes' own insect buzz, so deep a cry!
No ears.
No sounds.
Dawn breaks by the eyes' night.

시인의 마음

시인은 절도 살인 사기 폭력
그런 것들의 범죄 틈에 끼어서
이 세계의 한 모퉁이에서 태어났다

시인의 말은 청계천 창신동 종삼 산동네
그런 곳의 욕지거리 쌍말의 틈에 끼어서
이 사회의 한 동안을 맡는다

시인의 마음은 모든 악과 허위의 틈으로 스며나온
이 시대의 진실 외마디를 만든다
그리고 그 마음은
다른 마음에 맞아죽는다

시인의 마음은 이윽고 불운이다

A poet's heart

A poet is born in a chink of crimes,
larceny, murder, fraud, or violence,
in some obscure corner of the world.

First the poet's words go creeping
into chinks in harsh cursing's foulest oaths
heard in a city's poorest roughest slums,
and for a time dominate society.

Then the poet's heart fashions a single cry
out of all today's truths as they come seeping
through chinks in the evil and lies,
and gets beaten to death by other hearts.

A poet's heart is doomed, that's sure.

각혈(喀血)

1

아아 저물기 전에 노래하자
괴로움을
또한 첫눈을 노래하자

한 마리의 밤새가 되어
대낮 가득히 노래하자

2

아무리 바라보아도 어제의 하늘일 뿐
저 하늘에서는
눈이 내리고 내 가슴에서는 눈 쌓인다

아아 저물기 전에 노래하자 혼자도 괴로우면 여럿이구나

3

아아 저물기 전에 노래하자 저물기 전에 노래하자
나는 누구한테도 사랑받을 수 없고
오직 눈먼 산 보며 사랑하였다
아아 첫눈이 내리므로 노래하고 쓰러지자

Spitting Blood

1

Sing now, sing before sunset
songs of pain
songs of winter's first snow.

Sing now, as a bird of darkest night sings
to fill the bright daylight.

2

Gaze as I may, the sky is no different
from yesterday's sky.
Now snow comes falling, deep drifts in my breast.

Sing now, sing before sunset. I suffer alone
but lonely suffering makes me many.

3

Sing before sunset. Sing, before sunset.
I could get no love from anyone.
I gazed at the indifferent mountains and loved.
Early snow is falling; sing, then drop.

산사감각(山寺感覺)

높디높은 잠자리
차라리 울음
내 이마에도 울음
하늘이 진다
어느 바람자락 없이도
아니 바람 생각 없이도
잎새가 진다

그리하여 처음으로 트이는 소경의 눈으로
빈 마음이
빈 마음을 낳는다

저 노승(老僧)의 등에 진 하늘 속에 들어 있는
노승의 내일

가을 높디높은 풍경소리
차라리 밤!

Mountain temple sensations

High lofty dragonfly
no, tears falling
and on my brow, tears,
the sky is falling.
No breath of wind,
no thought of wind,
leaves are falling.

With the eyes of a blind man
seeing now for the first time,
an empty heart
gives birth to an empty heart.

That old monk's future
lies in the sky borne on his back.

High lofty autumn wind-bell,
or night falling!

여름 강가에서

하늘 아래서 강은 하늘을 낳는다
여름 강가에 나가
물푸레나무 손풍금소리를 듣는다
강은 저 홀로 깊어지지 않는다
항상 저 홀로 있으나 누가 그리워하게 한다
다른 나라에서도 여기까지 온 빛과 소리
강이야말로 이 세상에서 가장 좋은 길이다
저마다 한 굽이 한 굽이의 귀의(歸依)로서
얼마나 눈부신 잠이 되는가
이윽고 잠의 잔치인 강가에
여름의 기나긴 아름다움이여 소년이여 소녀들이여
그대들의 둘레를 거룩한 해으름 쌓이는 것은
그대들의 동정(童貞)의 타는 금빛이 강물에 실려 떠나기 때문이다
여름 강물이 이렇게 흐르듯이
이 세상 소년의 역사도 그렇게 흐를 수 있다면
이 강을 건너간 나그네들 다시 오지 않아도 된다
이 세상의 노을은 그대들의 것이며
밤이면 밤마다 새로운 별을 비춰주는 이 있으리라
하늘 아래서 강은 하늘을 낳는다
소년이여 소녀들이여 그대들의 손풍금소리
이 강은 공적(公的)으로 깊고 강 건너 그대들의 마을이
밤의 부유(富裕) 여름밤 하늘의 잔치로 드넓어지지라

A river in summer

Beneath the sky, a river brings the sky to birth.
Out by the summer river,
I hear concertina sounds in ash-trees.
The river will never get any deeper flowing alone.
Always alone, it yet makes others yearn so.
With light and sounds brought even from other lands
the river is the best road in the world.
By its returnings, curve upon curve,
what dazzling sleep it becomes, for sure.
Summer's long-drawn beauty, boys, girls,
on river banks soon to be a festival of sleep,
such mounds of glory shine around you because
the bright gold of your virginity floats away.
If this world's young history can really flow
as a summer river flows, travellers
who have crossed this river need never return.
This world's twilight glow is all yours,
someone will every night give new stars for light.
Beneath the sky, a river brings the sky to birth.
Boys, girls, your concertina sounds!
The river grows deeper by company
and on the other bank your village will expand
by night's abundance, a summer night sky's festival.

사치(奢侈)

어린 시절 고향 바닷가에서 자주 초록빛 바다를 바라보았
습니다
　그 바다가 저에게 자꾸 달려오려고 애를 썼으나
　저는 조금씩 물러날 뿐 마중 나가지도 못하고 바다는 바
다일 뿐이었습니다.
　빨랫줄은 너무 무겁게 팽팽해지고 마른 빨래는 날아가기
도 했습니다
　저 세상의 깃발인 빨래와 이 세상의 몸인 바다로
　제가 가지고 있던 오랜 병은
　착한 우단 저고리의 누님께 옮겨 갔습니다
　아주 그 오동꽃의 폐장(肺臟)에 묻혀 버리게 되었습니다
　누님은 이름 부를 남자 하나가 없고
　오직 〈하느님!〉〈하느님!〉만을 부르고 때로는 아버지도
불렀습니다
　저는 파리한 몸으로 누님의 혈맥에 흐르는 갈대밭의 애내
(欸乃)를 들었습니다
　이듬해 봄이 뒤뜰에서 머물다 떠나면
　어쩌다 늦게 피는 꽃에 봄이 남아 있었습니다
　백철쭉꽃이야말로 여름까지도 이어졌습니다
　이윽고 여름 한동안 저는 흙을 파먹기도 하며 울기도 했
습니다
　비가 몹시 내리고 마을 뒤 넓은 간석농지는 홍수에 잠겼
습니다

Luxury

As a child on the beach at home I often gazed
at the emerald sea.
Waves pounded toward me,
I only drew back, unable to meet them
and the sea remained simply the sea.
The laden clothes-line stretched heavily,
      the dry washing flapped and flew.
At last the disease I had long been carrying,
born of the washing (the other world's flags)
      and the sea (this world's body)
infected my gentle velvet-jacketed sister.
It was buried for good in the lungs of paulownia
      flowers.
My sister had no boy whose name she could call,
she only called "God! God!" or sometimes Father.
With my skinny body I heard a sobbing,
a field of reeds rustling in my sister's veins.
The next spring lingered in the backyard then left, yet
still spring remained in some late-blooming flowers.
White rhododendrons kept it until summer came.
All through the summer I simply ate dirt and cried.
The rains poured down and the broad salting farmlands
behind the village were flooded deep.

집이 둥둥 떠내려가는 온종일의 물 세상
누님께서 더욱 아름다왔기 때문에 가을이 왔습니다
그렇습니다 진정코 누님이야말로 가을이었습니다
찬 세면물에 제 푸른 이마 잔주름이 떠오르고
세수를 하고 나면 가을은 마치 하늘이 서서 우는 듯 했습
니다
멀리 기적소리는 확실하고 그 위에 가을은 한 번 더 깊었
습니다
잎진 나무에 겨우 몇 잎새만 붙어 있을 때도
그것은 사람에게 빈 나무이게 하고
누님은 그 잎새들과 더불어 이야기했습니다
기역자나 니은자 없이도 새소리 없이도 곧잘 말했습니다
그리고 맑은 뜰 그 땅 밑에서 뿌리들도 제대로 놀고 있었
습니다
하늘 역시 이 세상인 듯 하늘나라임에 틀림없고
그 하늘이 소리치며 더 푸르기 때문에 제가 눈 빠는 버릇
이 자고
어디서인지 제 행선지가 재삼재사 저를 기다리고 있었습
니다
누님께서 기침을 시작한 뒤 저는 급격하게 삭막하였습니다
차라리 제 턱을 치켜들어 삼라만상을 우러러 보아도
다만 제 발등은 움쩍도 않고 노쇠로 복수받았습니다

Houses floated by all day long in a world of water,
Autumn came because my sister grew more beautiful.
Really. Yes, truly. Sister was the cause of autumn.
As I washed in cold water wrinkles covered my green brow
and after I washed, the autumn pretended to be the sky,
              standing there crying.
Then a far away whistle would sound boldly and at that
autumn would grow deeper still.
Even when a few rare leaves were left on the trees
which made them bare trees for other people,
my sister would talk with those leaves.
She spoke quite well, without alphabet or bird-song.
And all the while, just below the ground of water-clear
gardens, roots were frolicking as they should.
The sky pretended to be our world, it was really Heaven
and because it shouted as it grew even bluer,
I gave up washing my eyes, for somewhere out there
my destination was all the while waiting for me.
Once sister started to cough, I suddenly grew sad.
I threw back my head and stared at all of Nature's works
yet my foot did not stir, I was avenged by senility.
Sister coughed blood until I could not endure it,
              and could not lament it.

마침내 제가 참을 수 없게, 울 수도 없게 누님은 피를 쏟았습니다

한 아름의 치마폭으로 그 피를 껴안았습니다 쓰러졌습니다

그때 저는 비로소 보았습니다 누님의 깊은 내부가 외부임을

그리고 그 동정(童貞)안에 내재하는 조석(潮汐)의 고향 바다를

그 뒤로 저의 잠은 누님의 시든 잠이었습니다

누님의 방에는 산 자 죽은 자의 고막으로 가득 찼고

저는 문 박에서 숱한 밤을 한 발자국씩 새웠습니다

누님께서 우단 저고리를 갈아입던 날

저는 누님의 황홀한 시간을 더해서

겨울 간사지 개펄을 헤매다가 돌아왔습니다

이듬해 봄의 음력 안개방울 달린 빈 빨랫줄을 가리키며

누님의 흰 손은 떨어지고 이 세상을 하직했습니다

저는 울지 않고 그의 흰 도자(陶磁) 베개 가까이 누워

얼마만큼 그의 죽음을 따라가다 돌아왔습니다

관 속은 누님인지 나인지 또는 어떤 기쁨인지 모르는 어둠이었습니다

She bundled the blood up in her skirt. She collapsed
That day I saw. Sister's inner being was there outside,
in her virginity lay the ebb and flow of the nearby sea.
After that my sleep was my sister's withered sleep.
Her room was full of the eardrums of quick and dead,
I watched outside her door as night went plodding by.
The day that she took off her velvet jacket,
I walked out and back along the winter shoreline
with my sister's hours of ecstasy prolonging.
Early the following spring my sister's pale hand dropped,
pointing to the empty clothes-line spangled with mist
and she bade the world farewell.
I did not cry; I lay close against her china-white pillow
and followed her death for a while, then returned.
In her coffin the dark was unsure whether it was sister
or I, or some kind of joy.

강은 흘러도

가을 볕 한 줌 쥔 시린 손 속으로
어린 것을 재울까

자장 자장이라는 무한한 위안이여
너를 재울 때
내 몸도 함께 재운다

내 딸이라 하여
강가 나룻배로
실어가고 싶은 맑은 날의 도둑

아무리 강은 흘러도
나는 그냥 강과 남남으로 있을 뿐이다

강가에서
어린 것처럼 어린 게 어디 있을까

The river may flow

Can I rock this baby to sleep
in these cold hands full of autumn light?

Now I'm rocking you to sleep
lullay, lullay, what a comfort!
I'll rock myself to sleep with you.

I feel like a thief in broad daylight,
pretending that you're my daughter.
I'd love to carry you off on a boat!

The river may flow,
it remains as ever a stranger to me.

A child looks most truly childlike
at the riverside.

애마(愛馬) 한스와 함께

오늘 새벽 수수잎새 같은 옷을 서걱서걱 걸치고
나는 4세 마(四歲馬) 한스를 타자 마구 달렸다
처음 콩밭 곡식을 거둔 빈 밭에는 채일 것이 없다

내가 달릴 때 말이 먼저 물 건너 종소리를 들었다
그리고 내 귀는 말의 귀에 대여져 어렴풋이 들었다

아직 주홍 꽃신을 제 품에 안고 내 외동딸은 쌕쌕거리겠지
내가 돌아와서, 네가 처녀가 되어 있으면 첫째 한스가 놀
라리라

어느덧 우리는 하얀 띠의 길을 달리는구나
말 고삐를 낚아채지 않아도
한스는 내 마음을 이미 알고 있다

새벽 길은 남은 가을 끝이 여기저기 잠들었고
침착하기 짝이 없는 대기(大氣)뿐, 캐비지밭을 덮고 밤은
지새었구나

모처럼 외동딸을 두고 어린 시절의 마을 장님 노래와
대만까지는 이틀이면 갈 바다와 박쥐들과……
내 한스는 그런 것을 내게 주면서 갈기 세워 달린다

56

Journey with Hans

At daybreak today I pulled on rustling clothes
dry like millet leaves, then mounted four-year-old Hans
     and off we sped, galloping at random.
The soy-bean field first: empty now, the crop long gathered.
     Nothing there to get in our way.

We galloped on. The horse heard it before me:
     a bell ringing across the stream.
Then my ears heard it faintly
     echoing in the horse's ear.

I suppose my darling daughter is breathing lightly,
     tightly hugging her scarlet shoes.
Hans would be the first to be surprised
     if she has grown into a girl by the time we return.

Suddenly there we were
     galloping down a white ribbon of road!
Hans always knows my thoughts,
     I never even need to twitch the reins.

Here and there along the early morning road
     relics of autumn lay dozing,

어디로 가느냐 내 두 다리를 말의 옆구리에 맡길 따름
그러면 한스는 새벽꿈이 주인 때문에 끊겼다고 투덜대다
가 만다

몇 십 년 동안 농부는 밭에 있건만 새벽 밭이라 빈 밭이
다
지난 여름 밤, 깊은 밤 곰별 자리 밑으로 한스는 멈춘다
내가 앞으로 가슴이 밀리다가 내리고 안장은 따뜻한 채
기다리리라
그러나 파리가 뜯어먹은 흉터쟁이 한스야 우리는 곧 돌아
가자꾸나
이제 신 한 짝이 품에서 내려지고
외동딸이 깨어 절망한 아침이구나
여기서는 잠깐 멈추자
잠깐 멈추는 곳도 중대한 곳이 아니냐

nothing but the air, unequalled in competence,
      and night, snug under the cabbage-field, lay waking.

Reluctantly I left my darling girl at home
      with a set of my childhood village blind man's songs,
the sea that would bring us in two days to China,
      the bats … Hans gallops on, his mane erect
      giving me all these things.

Where are we going? I entrust my legs to the horse's flanks.
Suddenly he complains that I, his boss,
      have interrupted his morning dreams!

The daybreak fields are empty though a farmer
      may spend years by the dozen working in them.
One night last summer, very late it was
      Hans came to a halt beneath the Great Bear.
I was jolted forwards, dismounted.
Your warm saddle will surely wait, I thought.

But scar-faced Hans, pestered by flies,
      quick, let's get home!

Now one shoe has dropped from her grasp
    and my daughter wakes. Early despair!
Let's pause here just for a moment:
    isn't a place to pause important, too?

On a woodland road at nightfall

The Evening Star rose earlier than normal;
     I managed to finish my work.
Our horse had gone smashing through the wind-break
then galloped all over the buckwheat field
     and messed it up as if he were scattering a crowd
so I had to go, dragging the horse along with me
     to make apologies to the field's owner.
But doing a bit of wrong is a beautiful thing, really.
On my way I may meet unexpected sorrows.

The owner's house lies up in the hinterland
     beyond the chestnut grove.
The pale field stands out more clearly once the sun has set!
I do not scold the horse as it trots along behind me,
only murmur in a low voice as we follow the woodland road.
Now we're nearly there. If you become a bit humbler,
I'll be your companion in humility, we'll grow old together.

At the entrance to the chestnut grove
     someone seems to come looming up behind us.
I keep looking back
     but total darkness is nudging at the horse's tail.
The nightfall woodland road is full of traces of the field's owner

저녁 숲길에서

어느 날보다도 일찍 미자르별이 뜨고 나는 겨우 일을 마쳤다.
우리 말이 방풍지대 너머로 달려 가서
해산(解散)하는 듯한 메밀밭을 버려 놓았기 때문에
나는 말을 끌고 밭 주인한테 사과하러 가야 한다.
그러나 한 두 번 잘못하는 일은 아름다움 아니랴
내가 가는 것은 뜻밖의 슬픔이라도 만나러 가는 것이 아니랴

밭 주인네 집은 밤나무숲 저쪽의 오지에 있다.
하얀 메밀밭은 저문 뒤에 더욱 역력하구나.
나는 뒤에 끄덕끄덕 따라오는 말더러 핀잔을 주지 않고
오직 숲길로 접어들자 중얼거림으로 말했을 뿐이다.
이제 다 왔다. 네가 좀더 겸손해지면
나도 너와 함께 겸손한 식구로 늙어가겠다라고

우리가 밤나무숲으로 들어가자 누가 뒤에서 일어서는 듯하다.
자꾸 돌아다보아도 말 꼬리에 채이는 것은 벌써 참된 어둠이다.
저녁 숲길은 밭 주인의 자취로 가득하고
나는 탄주(彈奏)하는 주인에게 할 말을 연거푸 궁량해본다.
잘못했습니다, 우리 말은 히잉히잉 운 뒤 몹시 후회하였

so I try to think of all the different things I'll say
        in response to the owner's performance.
We did wrong. Our horse was full of remorse,
he whined for a whole while afterwards.
But the owner who won't be angry
        isn't back yet.
Or rather the owner who will be angry
        isn't back yet.

I stroke his youngest daughter's hair.   .
How odd! My apologetic gesture hardens
        against the child's head.
Moss will grow on this child's tongue
        and she'll die.
Not able to meet the owner I take my leave.
A smell of rotting greens pursues us
until we have left the woodland house far behind.
My steps keep slipping,
the horses' long face exudes sorrow.
Death exists, how can we ever think
        of offering it some kind of polite apologies?

Now back quickly towards the south-west

습니다, 라고
　　그러나 화 내지 않을 주인은 아직 돌아오지 않았다.
　　아니 화 낼 주인도 돌아오지 않았다.

　　다만 밭 주인네 막내딸 머리를 쓰다듬어 주었다.
　　이상하구나 내 사과하는 손길이 그 아이 머리에서 굳어진다.
　　아무래도 그 애의 혀에 이끼가 끼며 곧 죽으리라.
　　나는 주인을 만나지 못한 채 그 집을 하직하였다.
　　그 숲 속의 집에서 너무나 멀리까지 야채 썩은 냄새가 따
라온다.
　　내 걸음은 훨씬 헛디딤이 잦고 말 얼굴도 더 길쭉하게 슬
픔을 뿌리친다.
　　죽음이 있다니 그 죽음에게 어찌 작은 사과를 하랴.

　　어서 나는 서남방으로 늙은 말과 돌아가야 한다.
　　서로 오래 일해 온 사이의 정으로 말과 나는 한 마음이다.
　　오던 길이 아니었다. 내 눈은 오던 길을 사납게 찾건만
　　그러나 낯선 길에서 말과 내 마음은 쭈뼛거리며 모지는
구나
　　말도 나와 너나들이 사이 오과부(吳寡婦) 흉내를 내며 따
라온다.
　　어디선가 개울물소리가 혼자 중얼거리는지
　　단 한 번 죽을 까치의 삶이 별빛처럼 까치소리를 낸다.

I and my aged horse.
My horse and I, united by work long shared together,
        have a single heart.
This wasn't the way we came. My eyes seek wildly
for the path we came by, on the unfamiliar road
        our hearts shudder grimly.
The horse follows tamely behind me,
imitating the closeness of old Widow Oh.
A stream can be heard murmuring somewhere alone.
The life of a magpie that one day must die
        is uttering magpie calls like starlight.
Sorrow, pain, or sin must stay
        close to the sound of the stream.

We're nearly there now.
Apologizing for my fault was not a problem
        but the little girl will die
I murmur almost inaudibly but at once the horse's rump droops.
This world's work is all touched close with death.
The road we follow returning
from our journey to apologize, is touched
        by smells of trees and earth.
The darkness inside the evening woodlands

슬픔일지라도 아픔일지라도 죄일지라도 개울물소리 가까이 맡기자

이제 다 왔다. 네 잘못 빌 처지가 아니라 그 애는 죽으리라
내가 겨우 들리도록 말하자 말은 엉덩이를 낮춘다.
이 세상 일은 다 죽음과 닿아 있고
우리들이 사과하러 갔다 오는 길에도 나무냄새 흙냄새로
닿아 있다.
저녁 숲속은 어둠이 바다 사릿때로부터 돌아온다.
마지막까지 낙조의 빛을 보내어 정성을 다하여
밭 주인네 딸의 죽음이 몇 번인가는 숨바꼭질도 되는구나.

어느 날보다 일찍 북돋기 일을 마치고 우리는 하루를 아
무린다.
우리가 돌아오는 길은 이제 밭 주인네 집에서 한참이나
멀어지고
이상하다. 내일 일들은 큰 강의 많은 지류가 되어 떠오르
지 않는다.
내가 갑자기 어느 영전(靈前)에 선 것같이 말이 느끼는지
오늘밤에는 제 마굿간에서 조금이라도 나와 함께 있기를
바란다.
마굿간은 참 잘 손질이 되었으니 정결한 말 뱃가죽냄새
뿐이다.

is returning from the sea's high tide.
Look! The owner's little daughter's death
        is out playing hide-and-seek
taking leave of twilight's last glimmerings,
        in all sincerity.

With the digging finished earlier than usual,
        the day is over now.
We have come a long way down a strange road
        from the house of the field's owner.
Tomorrow's jobs now fail to come to mind
        they are the many tributaries of some great river.
My horse seems to feel that we are standing
        before a departed soul,
tonight it wants me to stay for while, at least,
        the two of us together, in its stable.
The stable is well-kept, the only smell comes
        from the horse's belly.
Hurry up! From the house comes a splashing sound.
        Someone is washing.

어서 가자. 집에서 누가 몸 씻는 물소리가 난다.

그 위의 하늘 이웃에서는 들대로 든 정의 미자르별이 떠
기다리리라.

Hunting sunlight *

There's a young bride in every house
very much looked forward to!
Turning aside I made a long detour.
An old horse hears thunder in advance
well before the lightning strikes.
The world has been going on for far too long!
Sunlight comes vaulting over the mountains,
dropping from the sky, and now I have arrived.
Leave the village behind you
cross the fields of giant pearly onions;
there the sunlight is gathered.
We race as hard as we can to get there
yet it's always just beyond our reach.

Brides, you are one, yet you are many.
Close your eyes, look, there is sunlight.
You are waiting, there in the distance,
but the paths that I followed
as I came back from far away have vanished.
Here you are tearing
seven million and twenty thousand moments
one by one from my life full of screams.

햇빛사냥

집집마다 신부가 있다. 얼마나 기다렸느냐.
나는 제 길을 두고 멀리멀리 원주(圓周)를 돌아왔다.
늙은 말이 천둥소리를 미리 알 때
비로소 히뜩히뜩한 번개가 떨어진다.
아 이 세상은 너무나 오래되었다.
그리하여 햇빛이 산 넘어 하늘에서 오고
이제 내가 왔다. 마을을 벗어나서
여의주 양파 밭을 넘어가면
그곳이다. 모든 햇빛이 모여 있는 곳은
아무리 그대와 내가 달음박질쳐도
겨우 이르는 곳은 좀더 못미치는 곳이다.

신부여 단 하나라도 수많은 신부여
눈 감아라 햇빛이다. 햇빛이다.
저 멀리에서부터 그대는 기다리고
내가 멀리 돌아온 길들이 사라졌다.
이곳에서 그대가 7백 2만 크샤나의 순간들을
내 아우성의 일생에서 빼어버린다.

어느 나라에도 없다. 이 팽팽한 줄의 햇빛은 없다.
햇빛이여 햇빛과 하나가 된 신부여
그대는 영영 늙지 않고 빛난다.
어둠도 별도 다 없앤 삶으로

No other country has these taut rays of sunlight.

Look at the sunlight!

Brides, become one with the sunlight!

May you shine bright for ever, and never grow old.

Bright sunlight brides

your lives are free of darkness and stars.

My whole life long, I have taken aim and shot at you.

Note

* Seven million and twenty thousand moments: One twenty-four hour day
is made up of this many *ksana* in Buddhist thought.

71

빛나는 햇빛 신부
마침내 나는 그대를 겨눠 필생(畢生)으로 쏘았다.

Discipline and after

A few days ago
one of the dead came back from the tomb.
Wearing the same old smile,
with his everyday clothes restored from the ashes,
he gave quite a complete account of himself.
All around was full of light in water.
He said what he wanted to say
          then left like a letter.
My younger brother,
his heart and body polished pure,
saw him off standing close beside me.

We spend every afternoon like this now
          welcoming and saying goodbye.
Occasionally I hear talk from the dead
          of the Korea of centuries past.
They usually leave out a few things, I think.
After all, how could they say everything
          in one brief resurrection?
Their life's story, before and after they died,
is more than a few words can tell.

After seeing them off, my brother is silent

수행 여백(修行 餘白)

며칠 전에 죽은 사람이 무덤으로부터 왔다.

다 태워 버린 평상복을 그 재로부터 살려 내어 입고 옛 웃음 그대로

그는 자초지종을 이야기한다. 그 둘레는 물속의 빛이 어린다.

이야기를 실컷 한 뒤 그는 편지처럼 떠난다.

내 곁에서 몸 마음을 깨끗이 닦은 아우가 그를 보낸다.

언제나 오후에는 맞고 보내는 일을 한다.

고조선 때의 죽은 사람도 때때로 맞아들여 이야기를 듣는다.

그들은 으레 몇 가지는 빠뜨렸으리라.

잠깐 부활해서 어찌 모든 것을 다 말할 수 있겠는가.

살아 있던 때의 일 죽은 뒤의 일은 몇 마디 이야기 이상이다.

그들을 보내고 난 다음 아우는 놓은 그릇처럼 정숙하다.

긴 복도에 투명유리의 금기가 깔리고

언제나 그는 한 벌 홑옷만으로 저승 손님을 맞는다.

그의 말은 늘 나지막한 소리의 대꾸일 따름

혼자서 무엇이든지 받는 마음은 넓다.

언제나 오후에는 저승 손님을 맞고 보내는 일을 한다.

창밖의 햇빛은 해 시계, 그 시계로 때를 알고

like an empty bowl just lying there.
He always welcomes our visitors from beyond the tomb
wearing the same unlined clothes.
Eerie taboos of transparent glass
      spread along the corridor.
Responding simply in a quiet voice
      to what they say,
his heart is open, ready to receive everything, alone.

We always spend the afternoons welcoming
and taking leave of guests from beyond the tomb.
The sunlight beyond the windowpane is a sundial
      by which we tell the time.
Each word my brother hears from the dead
is first dried in the sun, then kept in reserve.
How very true! This world is the other world,
this world is the tomb, huge and vast.
Tomorrow, let's not say goodbye to those that come,
let's have them stay and live with us.

아우는 죽은 사람들이 들려준 이야기들을
한 마디씩 햇빛에 잘 말려서 둔다.
그렇구나 마침내 이 세상이 크나큰
저 세상이며 무덤이구나.
내일부터는 온 손님을 돌려보내지 말고 함께 살자.

2

섬진강에서

뼈저리거든 저문 강물을 보아라.
내가 은연중 불러도 가까운 산들은 밝은 귀로 내려와서
더 가까운 산으로
강들 위에 진하게 떠오르지만
또한 저 노고단 마루가 꽃처럼 떠오르기도 한다.
그러나 강물은 저물수록 저 혼자 진간장으로 흐르는구나.

뼈저리게 서럽거든 저문 강물을 보아라.
나는 그냥 여기 서서
산이 강물과 함께 저무는 큰 일과
그보다는 강물 가장자리 서러운 은어떼 헤매는 일과
화엄사 각황전 한 채를 싣고 흐르는 일들을 볼 따름이구나.

저문 강물을 보아라. 한동안을 즈믄 동안으로 보아라.
강물 위에 절을 지어서
그곳에 피아골 벽소령 죽은 이들도 다 모여서
함께 저무는 이 세상의 강물을 보아라.

강물은 흐르면서 아슬아슬 추위로 깊어진다.
나는 그냥 여기 서서
강물이 산을 버리고 산기슭 복사꽃 몇백만 심봉사 버리고
또한 커다란 절을 버리기까지
저문 섬진나루 강물을 눈 팔지 못하고 볼 따름이다.

Beside Somjin River

Does your heart ache?
Look at the river at nightfall.
I call in a low voice, the nearby hills are sharp-eared
they come dropping down and float there
nearer now, hills dark on the river water.
Even Mount Chiri's high ridge, Nogodan,
floats there like a drifting flower.
But look how the river flows on
all alone, a dark soja flood
in the deepening twilight.

Does your heart ache with sorrow?
Look at the river at nightfall.
I stand and watch.
Hills and river grow dark together;
greater still, tiny fish
drift in swarms close to the banks;
the river flows on, bearing away
one wing of Hwaom Temple's Enlightenment Hall.

Look at the river at nightfall.
Look! For a moment, a thousand years
see how this world's river builds a temple
floating on the water and grows dark

이제 살아 있는 것과 죽은 이가 하나로 되어
강물은 구례(求禮) 곡성(谷城) 누이들의 계면조 소리를 내
는구나.
그리하여 강 기슭의 이쪽 저쪽 어둠이 되고
그 어둠의 제자리로 높게 솟아올라
끝까지 빛나는 저 노고단마루도 문득 새소리 따위를 낸다.
살아 있는 사람 앞에서 강물은 이렇게 저무는구나.
보아라 만겁 번뇌 있거든 저문 강물을 보아라.

in union with all the people once murdered
in these valleys and hills.

The river water goes flowing on
deeper with the bitter cold.
I stand here watching. I cannot tear my eyes
away from the nightfall river at Somjin Ferry.
At last the river throws off the hills
throws off the millions of old blind men
the peach blossoms in the foothills
throws off at last the temple's bulk.

Things that live, things that have died
have now all become as one.
The river echoes the laments
of women from the nearby hamlets.
Now the shores have grown into darkness
but towering aloft, night's proper home,
the ridge of Nogodan shines on, bright to the end
uttering sudden sounds of birdsong and such.
So this is how the river water darkens
if someone is watching.
If you have endless ages of pain to spare,
look at the river at nightfall.

투망(投網)

최근 나에게는 비극이 없다.
나 이제까지 지탱해 준 건 복(福) 따위가 아니라 비극이
었다.
어이할 수 없었다.
동해 전체에 그물을 던졌다.
울릉 너머 수수리목 지나서까지
왜지(倭地) 추전현(秋田縣) 바닷가까지 ……
처음 몇 번은 소위 보수적 허무를 낚아 올렸을 뿐
내 그물에서 새벽 물방울들이 발전(發電)했다.
휘잉! 휘잉! 깜깜한 휘파람소리
내 손이 타고 내 사대색신(四大色身)이 탔다.
그러나 나는 참나무 숯이 된 채
신새벽마다 그물을 던졌다.
비극 한 놈 용보다도 더 흉흉한 놈이냐!
이윽고 동해 전체를 낚아 올려서
동해안의 긴 바닷가 모래밭에 오징어로 널어 됐다.

한반도 권세여 아무리 다급할지라도 바로 이 비극만은 팔
지 말아라
내 오징어로 눈부시게 마르는 비극만은 안돼! 안돼!

Fishing net

These days I have no tragedy left.
It was tragedy kept me going, not good luck.
How could it be otherwise?
All over the Eastern Sea I cast my net,
out beyond Ullong Island, past Susurimok,
        as far as the Japanese shore...
but all I caught at first
was so-called conservative nihility.
The early morning drops of water in my net
        sparkled electric.
A dark whistling came twanging
my hands and my body blazed
I was turned to oak-wood charcoal
and still I tossed my net with each new dawn.
The tragedy came by a bastard fiercer than any dragon!
Soon I had fished the whole Eastern Sea.
My catch lay drying like squid
        up and down the beaches there.

Dearest authorities, do not sell this tragedy!
No matter how great your need, not this one, please!
Not this tragedy drying dazzling here, bright as my squid!
You can't do it! No!

삼사경(三四更)

천 번 만 번 어두운 밤중
저 혼자 울부짖어서
꽃 한 송이는 핍니다.
그 옆에서
붉은 꽃 한 송이도 쇠벙어리로 핍니다.

The late watches

In thousand ten-thousandfold darkest night
one flower has bloomed
after screaming alone
and close beside it
a red flower has bloomed
speechless as iron.

살 생

어버이도 자식도 베허라
이것도 저것도 저것 아닌 것도
또 어떤 것도
어둠 속의 칼날로 베허 버려라
다음날 아침
천지는 죽은 것으로 쌓여서
우리 할 일은 그것들을 하루 내내 묻는 일

거기에 새 세상 세우는 일

Destruction of life

Cut off parents, cut off children!
This and that and this not that
and anything else as well
cut off and dispatch by the sharp blade of night.
Every morning heaven and earth
are piled with dead things.
Our job is to bury them all day long

and establish there a new world.

눈물 한 방울

내가 돌아다 보는 곳마다
어찌 내 눈물 한 방울 인색하겠느냐.
돌아다 보면
모든 가까운 것조차 멀리 있고
백운대나 오봉이
혹은 이 세상을 벗어난다.
늦가을 된장잠자리 한 마리도 위로하지 못하고 살아온 신세
지금 나에게는 산뿐 아니라
죽어가면서 끝까지 함께 있을 내 아내와 조국까지도
이 세상을 벗어나서
이 세상 저 세상의 바람소리 따라간다.
소루쟁이 풀 한 포기도 위로하지 못하고 살아온 신세
내 것만이 모두라고 허욕으로 살아서
내가 서 있는 곳에서
인천 앞바다까지는 죽어서나 가야 한다.
개울물 흘러가서 거기까지 남이 아니건만
개울물 한 굽이 왕십리 또랑물 하나도 위로하지 못한 신세
내가 돌아다 보는 곳마다
어찌 내 눈물 한 방울 인색하겠느냐.
이 세상은 돌아다볼 때
가장 세상다와서
나는 이 세상을 떠나기 싫다.
죽어가면서

A single teardrop

Why should I grudge a teardrop
for every place I look back on?
When I look back now,
even places nearby have moved a long way off;
the hills towering behind Seoul
seem to have almost quit the world.
It has been my lot in life
to have failed to bring any comfort
to even the humblest of autumn's dragonflies.
Not only the hills, but my wife and my country,
accompanying me along the way to death
are quitting the world now, following the sound
of the wind that gusts from this world to the next.
It has been my lot in life
to have failed to bring any comfort
to even the smallest clump of knotgrass.
I have lived with the vain desire
to take what was only mine for everything
and so from where I stand now I cannot reach
the coast at Inchon unless I die.
It has been my lot in life
to have failed to bring comfort
to even the humblest river

내 아내에게 맡기는 이 세상에서
결국 나라고 하는 한 마리 사람이란 아내의 눈물 한 방울
아내여 내가 돌아다보는 곳마다
실로 눈물겨운 것들이 태어난다.
죽어도 다시 태어나서
그대를 알아보는 이 세상이라면
어찌 그대와 함께 흘리는 눈물로
이 세상 갖은 슬픔 위로하지 않겠느냐.

even that ditch in the East End of Seoul
although it's no stranger to me
with all the river waters flowing into it.
So why should I grudge a teardrop
for every place I look back on now?
When I look back on this world
it's so much like itself
that I hate to leave it.
As I die
in this world that I bequeath to my wife
this so-called human being is no more
than one of my wife's teardrops.
From every place that I look back on
truly touching things are born, my dear.
I may die, but after I am born again
if I recognize you here
I know I shall comfort every sorrow
by my tears shed in harmony with yours.

이어도

아무도 이어도에 간 일이 없다.
그러나 누구인가 갔다 한다.
가서는 영영 돌아오지 않았다 한다.
이어도 어디 있나
물결 청동 골짜기
동남방으로 동남방으로
눈썹 불태우는 수평선뿐이다.
이어도 어디 있나.
제주 어부 핏속에 사무친 섬
아무리 노 저어도
돛 올려 내달려도
제주의 꿈 어디 있나.
이어도 어디 있나
성산 해돋이 장님의 섬
파도야 파도야 너뿐이다.
파도 온누리에 북을 울려라.
흰구름 일어나거라.
세찬 호니보름 오거라.
여기 어디냐
여기 어디냐
올 대로 와버린 바다 돌이킬 수 없다.
두고 온 딸의 울음소리
파도 속에 박혀 있다.

Eoh Island

No one ever went to Eoh Island.
They say someone went, though,
went and never came back.
But where is Eoh Island?
Down the waves' bronze valleys
south-east, south-east, lies
only the eyeball-searing horizon.
But where is Eoh Island?
Row as hard as you can
skim with all sails set!
Perhaps that island, Cheju's dream,
deep in its fishermen's blood,
lies somewhere near?
Where is Eoh Island, the blind man's island
glimpsed at sunrise over Songsan?
Waves, endless waves, alone
thunder on, waves, thunder to the world.
Arise, white clouds.
Mighty surf, come rolling.
But where are we?
Where are we?
The sea comes breaking, no return.
In the waves is hid the sound

제주 어업 몇천 년동안 이어도 어디 있나.
그러나 저기 있다.
저기 있다가 사라졌다.
이어도 어디 있나.
아무도 간 일이 없다.
그러나 누군가가 갔다.
가서 돌아오지 않을 뿐
저기 있다.
저기 있다.
아니다. 파도뿐이다. 숨막히는 파도뿐이다.

of my daughter crying, left behind.
Is Eoh Island anywhere near
the thousands of years spent fishing here?
It is there, though!
It was there, then it vanished.
Is Eoh Island anywhere near?
No one ever went there.
Yet someone went
went and will never come back again.
Oh it's there, for sure, it's there.
Oh no. Only waves.
Nothing but overpowering waves.

두만강으로 부치는 편지

누이여 회령 남양의 강 기슭에
회령 남양의 버들 같은 누이여 누이여
두만강 얼음덩어리 둥둥 떠가며 풀렸는가.
땅이야 무엇 한 가지 따로 갖지 않고 봄 오니
이 세상에 봄처럼 공평한 것 어디 있으랴.
누이여 자네 아이들 잘 있는지, 강도 더러 깊어졌는지
또 누이여 그대 얼마나 늙은 표라도 나는가.
말과 뜻이 한 다발로 잡아매어져도
여기서는 천하 군사분계선 아득한지라
그대 얼마나 옛모습의 뿐 남았겠는가.
이 땅에서 태어난 사람으로서는
이런 인사도 입에 발려서 헛되거니와
회령 남양의 해 저문 추운 강가에
차라리 인사불성의 버드나무들 잘 있는가.
누이여 자네도 오라비인 나도
우리 겨레에게는 웃음 하나도 적(蹟)으로 바치는 아픔 아
닌가.
백 번도 한 번도 내 누이인 누이여
자네 거기서 살다 죽고 나 여기서 죽어도
그런 무명인민의 죽음이 우리 겨레의 역대 삶이 아닌가.
누이여.

A letter sent to the Tuman River

Sister! My dear sister! Like the willows rising
along the riverside at Namyang, at Huinyong!
The willows up in Namyang and Huinyong, dear sister!
I wonder, has the ice covering the Tuman River broken?
Has it broken up booming and gone drifting away?
Here? Well, spring has come, nothing else,
yet when all's said and done,
what could be more like justice than spring?
I wonder, though, are your children well?
Has the river got any deeper?
How much older have you grown to look at?
My words and my will are bound tight together, but
far from where I stand lies a line dividing us.
How much remains of what you once looked like?
But what use such feelings bursting from the lips
of people like us who were born in this land?
I rather should ask if those unfeeling willows
along the cold river banks
at sunset in Namyang and Huinyong are well?
You as my sister, or I as your brother
or even a simple smile
can only be an aching sore for all of us.
My sister dear, one hundred times dear

ever dear, sister,
suppose that you die up there one day
and I down here? But that's our people's life,
age after age, that kind of hidden, nameless death.
My dearest sister!

My pony Eul Pa-so

As the night closes in, the road lies alert
like a guiding voice.
The road stretches far, wide awake for us.
Wounded Eul Pa-so, my pony!
Let's pursue our path, not hastening.
There's nothing we need regret.
Life in itself is never sublime
      it's the road we take
and the passing of time that make it sublime.
Dark across the sky a spider's web stretches
catching the starlight as it falls.
No, no one can ever address the stars,
no matter how powerful a voice they have.
All we can do is fill with night
the empty vessels piled rattling on our cart.
The road becomes more and more familiar,
as the busy tinkling of your bells
tinkling on through years of fruitlessness
sometimes drowzes on the journey.
Let's pursue our path, not hastening,
      old Eul Pa-so!
If our hearts are not too busy
the dark will duly stand aside

을파소(乙巴素)

밤이 깊어서 길은 소리처럼 깨어 있다.
우리를 위하여 멀리까지 깨어 있다.
다친 조랑말 을파소야
서둘지 않고 가자.
우리는 무슨 일에도 후회를 겸한 일 없다.
삶이란 아예 숭엄하지 않고
삶의 길과 세월로 숭엄해진다.
하늘에는 캄캄하게 거미줄이 자라고
때때로 별빛이 거기에 걸리며 내려온다.
아무리 큰 소리를 가진 사람도
별을 아무리 아무리 부를 수 없다.
우리는 흔들리는 수레에 실은
빈 그릇에 밤을 온통 담았을 뿐이다.
길은 더욱 몇 갑절로 친하여
네 부지런한 흉년의 방울소리는
지나는 길에서 잠들 때도 있다.
서둘지 말고 가자, 을파소야
마음이 지레 바쁘지 않으면
어둠은 차례로 비켜나서
우리가 온 뒤를 겸허하게 따라온다.
이제 바람 자는 풀밭길을 지나서
불 꺼진 외딴 마을과
자꾸 헛디디어지는 넓은 배추밭 길도 지났다.

then humbly follow on behind us.
Along meadow roads where breezes doze
we pass before lonely unlit homesteads
and wide cabbage-field roads
        where steps keep sliding.
An old man dying neither summons death nor shuns it;
so let's pursue our path, not hastening.
By the time day comes we'll be there.
Or the chill house will come rushing to meet us
after waiting a while at the end of the road.
So let's pursue our path, not hastening,
        old pony Eul Pa-so.
I regret my poverty must pay for your fodder:
you were born resolved to accept no gifts,
        I'm sorry.
The road turns everything sleeping into road
even the veiling night.
But why is everything here so familiar,
living, and dying, and the torments of youth?
        Old Eul Pa-so!
You know my heart too well!
Look! Passing in front of the sleeping pub
you slacken your pace and turn your eyes back!

죽어가는 노인 죽음을 서둘지도 피하지도 않고
우리도 서둘지 말고 가자.
먼동이 잘 틀 때까지는 도달한다.
그렇지 않으면 끝에서 기다리다가
추운 집이 달려오리라.
서둘지 말고 가자. 조랑말 을파소야
내 가난은 언제나 네 여물 대기도 딱한 적 있으나
아무것도 받지 않으려고 이 세상에 온 너에게 미안하다.
길은 잠든 것들이 둔 어둠까지도 길이게 한다.
왜 이렇게도 익숙한 것인지
삶도 죽음도 젊은 날의 괴로움도.
을파소야 너는 내 마음 잘도 알아서
잠든 술집 지나갈 때는
뒤를 돌아다보며 걸음을 늦추는구나.
그러나 지나가버리자.
밤이 깊으면 술보다 밤이 더 좋다.
내가 내 죽음이나 네 죽음 생각하면
너도 또한 내 죽음을 생각해 준다.
서둘지 말고 가자.
가서 네 마굿간 깨끗한 데서 쉬고
다음날 없이 죽는다 한들 어떻겠느냐.
을파소야 이제 절반 대중이 넘어
네 쉰 꼬리가 한 번 영(嶺)을 치는구나.

But let's go on past it now.

Dark night is better than any wine.

While I reflect on my death, or yours,

you reflect on mine.

Let's pursue our path, not hastening.

Suppose we went to rest in a clean place,

      your stall, say,

and died there, with never a thought of tomorrow?

Eul Pa-so, now we're more than half way there.

Look! already your withered tail's sweeping the ridge!

대장경

한반도야 한 이삼백 년만 푸욱 가라앉아라
그냥 바다밖에는 아무것도 없도록
아무리 찾아보아도
창천하(蒼天下) 바다밖에는 아무것도 없도록
그리하여 이 강토 삼천리를
대장경 원목으로 바닷물에 푸욱 절였다가
한 이삼백 년 뒤에 떠오르게 하라
눈보라 일월성진이야
그대로 지긋지긋하게 두고
한반도의 온갖 싸구려 권세 죽여서
빈 땅으로 두둥실 떠오르게 하라
거기 새 꽃 새 열매 나라 세우고
잃어버렸던 말을 찾아 말하게 하라
뭇사람의 진리 말하게 하라
그리하여 삭지 않는 대장경으로도 남아서
이제부터 거룩한 이는 뭇사람임을 말하라
한반도야 한반도야 이대로는 안되겠구나
매스게임 가라 매스게임 가라
사람을 사람답게 하고 뭇사람을 거룩하게 하라
한반도야 한 이삼백 년 아니거든
눈 딱 감고 막무가내로 천년만 가라앉아라

The Buddhist Scriptures carved in wood

If this land of ours would only sink beneath the sea!
Sink deep for, say, three hundred years, sink down
till nothing was left above the waves,
search as they might,
nothing under heaven's arch above the sea.
Then, once its whole length and breadth
had soaked for, say, three hundred years,
like the wood where Buddhist Scriptures were carved,
it could be raised up again.
Snowstorm, sun, moon, stars? Oh, let them stay put!
They can endure, unbearable.
If at last our Korean land
were brought floating lightly back to the daylight
an empty land,
all the country's tawdry powers dead,
a new nation might be established there,
one with new flowers, new harvests,
a land where they would speak a language
forgotten, then rediscovered.
Yes! And then declare the truth of all;
since the Scriptures remain intact, declare
that henceforth Everyone is the Holy One.
Korean Land! This present life will never do!

Away with mass-games! No more mass-games!
Treat people as people! All people as sacred!
Close your eyes, now, Korean Land,
sink firmly down for three hundred years!
If not, you'll have to sink down
for a full thousand years!

몰래 물어 보는 몇 마디 말

귀뚜라미야 너 밤마다
어둠을 썰어서 무엇하느냐
사람들의 잠도 다 썰어서
어디 시뻘건 피 흘리게 해보려마
이제 사람은 피도 흘리지 않고
그냥그냥 살아가려고만 하는구나
어느 산등성이 산사마귀 밭두렁에도
슬픈 피 흘리지 않은 데 없단다
귀뚜라미야 귀뚜라미야
찬 이슬에 흠뻑 술 취한 귀뚜라미야
이 나라 이슬 한 방울
어린 눈물 한 방울
어느 것도 다 피 아닌 것 없건만
앞 뒤에서 자는 잠 깊은 잠뿐이냐
지지리 못난 간이나 쓸개 꺼내어가도
숫제 모르는 무지렁이 잠뿐이냐
귀뚜라미야 귀뚜라미야
어둠도 썰고 잠도 썰어서
가을아침 무서리 된 서리 정신 하나 번쩍나거라

A secret question

Tell me, cricket, what do you think you're doing
night after night, slicing through the dark?
You slice through people's sleep too, you know.
Do you want scarlet blood to be shed?
Ah, nowadays people don't shed blood!
All they want is a quiet life!
Yet there's not an inch of ground,
not a single hill, not soaked in sad blood.
Cricket, old cricket,
rolling drunk on icy dew, friend cricket:
every last drop of this country's dew,
each single one of our children's tears
is all blood now, nothing but blood.
But everything lies asleep, sleep on all sides,
nothing but deep deep sleep.
Is there nothing left,
except ugly louts so fast asleep
they'd never once notice
if you cut out their guts, or their gall?
Cricket, old cricket, go on!
Slice through the dark, slice through sleep,
and jolt minds awake like autumn frost,
like an early, biting frost.

종 신(終身)

아네스수녀 종신수녀를 서원한다는 글월을 받고
바람끼 한 점 없는 마당의 후박나무를 본다
다 부동자세인 다른 것들도 시름겹게 본다
그래, 너희들이나 나도 요런 쇠뭉치 침묵 가운데서
뭔가를 번쩍! 종신서원해야겠구나
너희들은 해마다 그냥 나무잎새요
나 또한 날마다 비분의 탕아로다
서로 산과 들 건너 뛰어
아네스 숫처녀의 뜻과 우리 뜻이 하나 되면
올 가을에는 하늘의 곡식 별도
땅의 곡식도 그냥 이래저래서는 안 되겠구나
우리가 사는 이 역사에도 일망무제의 해일(海溢)이 밀려
와야겠구나

Perpetual vows

Receiving a card announcing
Sister Agnes's Perpetual Vows
I gaze out at the garden's camphor tree.
In the garden, no hint of wind!
Everything rigid and stiff. I'm afraid.
All of you, I too,
we all should make perpetual vows
and tear this stony silence apart.
Of course, you're mere annual leaves,
I'm a resentful Prodigal every day.
But if we race together over hills and fields,
blending Sister Agnes' resolve and ours,
then when autumn comes
the sky's harvest, stars,
and the earth's harvest of grain,
will not be everyday ordinary ones.
A tidal wave should come to flood
all this history in which we are living,
a flood of boundless abundance!

상원사(上院寺)에서

오대산 어둠이라는 건, 이건 어둠이 아니라 대혁신이다.
내가 어쩔 수 없이 이르노니 별들아
내 가슴에도
별밖에 들어 있는 것 없다.
내 가슴 극한으로
빛나는 별들아
이제 이 세상 새 세상의 때가 왔느냐.

별들아
별들아
때가 왔느냐. 빛나라

From Sangwon Temple

Odae Mountain's so-called night
is no mere night. It's total renovation!
Stars, I can't help it, I must say this.
Utter starlight has pierced my heart.
You stars shining so bright
at the farthest limits of my heart, tell me,
has the time come at last for this world's newness?

Stars!
Stars!
Has the time come at last? Shine on! Shine bright!

지구(地球) 놀이

어젯밤 나 딱한 여자한테 팔 하나를 잘라 줬다.
나 또 팔 하나를 뚝 잘라 줬다.
나에게는 팔이 없다. 허허허.

오늘 새벽 나는 이웃 놈팽이한테 다리 둘도 몽땅 잘라 줬다.
나에게 다리가 없다. 허허허
내가 생각하고도!
도무지 무슨 수작인지. 허허허

오늘 아침 나는 동물원 사자란 놈한테
몸통도 내 줘버렸다.
나한테는 이제
어깨쭉지도 배꼽도 없다.
허파도 지레 간 창사구도 없다. 허허허.

이제 별 수 없이 나는 대가리뿐이다.
대가리뿐이다.
대가리뿐이다. 허허허
내 머리를 조계사 대머리 중이 차 버린다.
나는 떠굴떠굴 잘도 굴러간다.
저쪽에서 다른 중대가리가 박치기한다.
나는 공중에 떠올랐다가
툭! 떨어졌다.

Games with a globe

Last night I cut off one arm
and gave it to a poor woman.
Then I cut off the other arm
--gave that to her too.
So now I have no arms. Haha.

Early this morning I cut off both legs
and gave them to a nearby idler.
I'm legless now. Haha.
I wonder though:
did I get anything back?

This morning I abandoned my torso
to a lion in the zoo.
So now I have
no shoulder-blades, no navel either.
No lungs, what's more, no spleen or liver. Hahaha.

It can't be helped, now I am nothing but a head,
nothing but a head,
nothing but a head. Haha.
A bald-headed monk from Chogye Temple
kicks my head away.

지구놀이다. 지구놀이. 허허허.

봐라. 내가 이 놈의 싸가지 없는 지구 전체를
단 한 번의 박치기로
우주 공전 자전 궤적에서 멋지게 일탈시켜 버릴 터!
그래서 아주 지구란 걸
우주의 어느 허공에 소실시킬 터!

Off I go spinning merrily.
Over there another shaved monk butts at me.
Up I soar high
then down I fall, plonk!
Global games! World games! Hahaha.

Just look at this!
With one single butt I can send the earth,
this mindless earth, this mischievous earth astray,
off course, off its tracks!
I can send this world off
to vanish for ever into some void of outer space!

다시 조계산에 들어가

1978년 여름 나는 강제로 송광사에 갇혀서
친구야 유폐라는 것 아느냐
한달 동안 밤 소쩍새소리 머리 썩으며 들었단다
시 한 조각 안썼다
조용히 쉬라고 서너달 쉬고 오라고 어쩌고……
시 대신 내 품에는 날 선 칼이 솟아올랐다
그 칼 어쨌느냐고? 친구야
어느 밤중 조계산 탈출할 때 내던지고 말았다

두번째로 나는 또 송광사에 갔다
흐르는 화엄전 물아 친구야
흐르지 말고 시퍼런 물기둥을 세워보아라

아 엄청난 모순 백년
이 나라의 모순 백년
이 때문에 나는 아직도 시인이어야 한다
시인아 누가 너를 약하다고 말하더냐
시인은 죽음까지도 합해서
역사에 산다
시인아 너는 강하다 네 자식이 말해주리라

Return to Chogye Mountain

All through the summer of '78
I was forced to stay confined
        in Songkwang Temple
and tell me, friend,
        isn't that called incarceration?
For one whole month
I listened to the nightbirds singing
        while my brain grew addled.
I wrote not a single poem.
Stay there and rest, they said,
stay there and rest for three or four months ···
Instead of poems a sharpened knife grew up
        in my breast.
And what became of that knife, you ask? One night,
as I made my escape from Chogye Mountain,
        I finally threw it away.

I went back to Songkwang Temple a second time.
You, friend stream at Hwaom Temple,
stop flowing; instead form a dark blue pillar of water.

What a century of fearful contradictions!
A century of contradictions for our land!

That's why I have to be a poet!
Tell me, poet: will people call you weak?
A poet, even when he dies,
lives in our history.
Therefore, poet, your children
will surely say you were strong.

For myself

Don't cover my eyes to shoot me!
I will die on my feet.
Unjustly accused in this beautiful land,
I will die on my feet!
I'll not call for my mother.
Or for anything else.
The more gruesome death is,
the more luxurious it is.
Death is no defeat,
no disgrace, or senility.
It should be a red flower,
a white hyacinth.
It should be that darkness of philosophy
that is like a cliff in deepest night.
Shoot now, shoot!
Five bullets from an M16,
then the coup-de-grace.
This is the only moment
in all our nation's history
when I can be an artist.
Shoot now!
Shoot!
Don't cover my eyes!

나 자신을 위하여

두 눈 가리지 말고 쏴라
나는
이 아름다운 나라의 누명을 쓰고
서서 죽겠다
서서 죽겠다
어머니를 부르지 않겠다
또 무엇도 부르지 않겠다
죽음은 처참할수록 화려하다
죽음은 패배가 아니라
오욕과 노쇠가 아니라
붉은 꽃
흰 히야신스여야 한다
한밤중 벼랑과도 같은 철학의 어둠이어야 한다
쏴라 쏴라
엠 16총탄 5발
확인사살 1발
내가 우리나라 역사 속에서
단 한 번 예술가일 수 있는 때는
이때뿐이다
쏴라
쏴라

I lived with my eyes,
with my eyes I'll die, young guardsmen!

두 눈 가리지 말고
눈으로 살아
눈으로 죽겠다 젊은 헌병이여

Arrows

Transformed into arrows
let's all go, body and soul!
Piercing the air
let's go, body and soul,
with no way of return,
transfixed there,
rotting with the pain of striking home,
never to return.

One last breath! Now, let's quit the string,
throwing away like rags
all we've had for decades
all we've enjoyed for decades
all we've piled up for decades,
happiness,
the lot.
Transformed into arrows
let's all go, body and soul!

The air is shouting! Piercing the air
let's go, body and soul!
In dark daylight the target is rushing towards us.

화 살

우리 모두 화살이 되어
온몸으로 가자
허공 뚫고
온몸으로 가자
가서는 돌아오지 말자
박혀서
박힌 아픔과 함께 썩어서 돌아오지 말자

우리 모두 숨 끊고 활시위를 떠나자
몇 십년 동안 가진 것
몇 십년 동안 누린 것
몇 십년 동안 쌓은 것
행복이라던가
뭣이라던가
그런 것 다 넝마로 버리고
화살이 되어 온몸으로 가자

허공이 소리친다
허공 뚫고
온몸으로 가자
저 캄캄한 대낮 과녁이 달려온다.
이윽고 과녁이 피 뿜으며 쓰러질 때
단 한 번
우리 모두 화살로 피를 흘리자

126

Finally, as the target topples
        in a shower of blood,
let's all just once as arrows
        bleed.

Never to return!
Never to return!

Hail, arrows, our nation's arrows!
Hail, Warriors! Spirits of the fallen!

돌아오지 말자
돌아오지 말자

오 화살 조국의 화살이여 전사여 영령이여

Early morning road

Mother!
First, you sold a few handfuls of scalded greens,
some bunches of radishes
from your vegetable basket.
Then, as your son was leaving home,
kicking the dew along the early morning road,
        mother,
you said, "Go up to Seoul and make good, really good!"
You gave him a ball of salted rice, and the fare.
Then, after your son had left home,
        mother,
you set the Seven Stars of the Great Wain
on your white hair, though those stars lost
their miraculous powers a thousand years ago,
and you prayed and prayed,
firmly fixed before a bowl of cold water,
        and mother,
thanks to all those prayers you said
your son became a drunken lout.
Seoul? Nothing but a foreign colony,
and then again, a new colony
where sunset is a rotten pumpkin sinking
into the lower reaches of the River Han!

새벽길

어머니
푸성귀 광주리 장수로 데친 비듬나물 몇 줌이나
콩밭김치거리 열무 몇 단 팔아서
어머니의 자식 새벽길 이슬 차며 떠날 때
서울 가서 으리으리 성공하라고
주먹밥 노잣돈 주신 어머니
어머니
어머니의 자식 떠난 뒤
천년이나 영검없이 빤짝거리는
북두칠성 흰 머리에 이고
찬물 한 그릇에 정들도록 빌고 빈 어머니
어머니의 자식은 그렇게 빈 덕택으로 술주정뱅이 되었습니다
일제 식민지의 서울
또다시 신식민지의 서울 한강 하류에
썩은 호박 해가 집니다
아니 양키 삼십여 년 하우스보이로 늙고 병들었습니다
술 마시면 수많은 역사 가지고
언제나 새로 태어난 가슴이나
다음날은 그 가슴에 구멍 뚫려
뚫린 구멍으로 지난날 새벽길 환히 보입니다
어머니
언제까지나 서낭당 마루에 서서
떠나는 자식 바라보시는 어머니 환히 보입니다

For thirty long years he served the Yanks,
grew old and sick working as their houseboy.
Whenever he drank there was so much to say,
and always a reborn breast, as well,
but when the next morning dawned, lo and behold,
there in his breast a gaping hole again,
and clearly visible through that hole
the early morning road of a day long ago.
　　　Mother
you can clearly be seen
gazing after your son as he goes on his way,
standing long on the village hilltop.
Now that's enough,
go back home to your mud-walled poverty,
don't keep counting off on your fingers
the days and the months,
waiting for your son to appear.
There was a blizzard,
a blizzard and a downpour.
　　　Your son became a drunken lout.
Not a rich man in a house
with twelve front doors,
only press a bell and it all gets done,

이제 그만 흙담집 가난으로 돌아가세요
이제 그만 어머니의 자식
해로써 달로써 손꼽아 기다리지 마세요
눈보라였습니다
눈보라 비바람이었습니다
어머니의 자식은 술주정뱅이입니다
천 사람의 권리 몽땅 먹은 권세
만 사람의 것 다 삼킨 부자
단추 하나 누르면
다 이루어지는 열두 대문집 아니어요
어머니의 자식은
아무것도 없이
아무것도 없이
문둥이 눈썹 다 빠지고
어머니의 자식 마흔살이 되어
어느날 술잔 꽉 쥐어 깨어 버리고
새 세상 같은 붉은 피 손바닥에 쥐었습니다
가슴팍도 이마빡도 들이받아 피흘렸습니다
더 이상 기다리지 말아야 합니다
오천 년을 기다려 온 그날
긴 긴 세월 오백 년으로 오십 년으로
아니 남과 북 허리 잘려서
총구멍 맞댄 세월

with powers that devour the rights of a thousand,
commandeering the goods of thousands more.
     Your son
has nothing,
nothing at all,
his leper's eyebrows are all gone too,
and when your son turned forty one day
as he roused himself from a drunken stupor
he smashed the glass in his open hand
     then grasped it,
blood flowed red, red as a new-made world.
He beat his breast and beat his brow,
the blood poured down. No,
he must not wait any longer now.
He must not wait, a drunken lout.
I have abolished the coming day,
that day awaited for five thousand years,
after such long ages, five hundred years, fifty years,
ages with South and North chopped in two at the waist,
rifle barrel to rifle barrel,
ages with this one and that one acting as puppet;
that day will come, it will certainly come,
if you only keep waiting -- I have quite abolished it.

이놈도 저놈도 앞잡이 세월에
그날이 오리라고
꼭 오리라고 견디어 온 그날 다 지워 버렸습니다
어머니
한 핏줄 서로 부둥켜 안을 그날이
가슴마다 가슴마다 해뜨는 그날이
언제냐고 묻지 마세요
어머니
술주정뱅이 어머니의 자식 이제야 싸움터로 갑니다
싸워야만 살 수 있는 싸움터로 갑니다
새벽길 찬바람 속에
두 주먹 불끈 쥐어 어머니의 주먹밥 만들었어요
가슴에 원한 서리고 서려
어머니의 노자돈 가득합니다
오늘 하루가 어머니의 오랜 세월입니다
먼동 찢어 새벽길 떠나며
날선 칼로 몸뚱이 되어
어둠 속에 잉걸불 되어
싸워서 그날을 등에 지고 오렵니다
피묻은 깃발 날리며
찢어진 깃발 휘날리며
다친 다리 칭칭 싸매고 그날을 지고 오렵니다
그날이 어머니의 자식입니다

Mother,
do not ask when that day will come,
that day when each family will be united
in one embrace,
when the sun will rise in every heart,
do not ask.
        Now mother's drunken loutish son
is on his way to the battlefield,
to the battlefield where only the fight
        can make life possible.
In the bitter wind on the early morning road,
with fists clenched I kneaded the ball of rice
        you gave me.
My heart is brimming full with bitterness,
full of that money you gave for the fare.
This present day is your long long waiting.
At break of dawn,
        setting out along the early morning road,
my body has turned into a sharpened knife,
turned into a blaze of fire in the dark;
after the fight I will return
with that day loaded on my back.
With a blood-stained banner waving,

135

그날이 모든 어머니의 자식입니다
어머니 아닙니다
젊은날 보리방아 찧을 적마다
쭉정이 젖통 출렁거리던 설움
어머니의 자식 죽어서
백골 한 자루로 그 젖 달라고 울부짖으렵니다
어머니
어머니의 자식 늙은 자식 싸움터에 가서
오천 년 역사의 그날 민족 하나 꼭 이루렵니다

that tattered banner streaming out,
with my wounded leg roughly bound up,
I will return, bearing that day.
That day is your son.
That day is every mother's son.
        No, mother, I can't say that.
I recall the sorrow of your blasted breasts
swaying as you pounded barley
in the days of our youth;
now your son has died
and reduced to blanched bones
whimpers for the milk of your sorrow again.
        Mother,
in his old age your son sets out for the battlefield
and surely that day will come,
sustained by five thousand years of history.
Our nation will be one.

대웅전

부처님 끌어내려요
잘 먹어 잘 생긴 부처님 끌어내려요
어쩌다가 간드러진 풀잎 수염은 왜 그 모양이어요
다음날
단청 똥갈보 대들보 내려요
용대가리는 무슨 용대가리예요
대웅전 다 허물어
중들 쫓아버리고 먼지구더기 돼 버려요
할!

없는 부처님 당신이 부처예요
욕 잘하는 청계천 우리 엄마가 부처예요
우리 모두 다 부처부처부처예요
산 부처 담배 한 대
떡 치게도 거룩한 부처예요

아니에요
만약 이 세상 떡판에 떡 차고
사람마다 떵떵거리며 잘 살아도
같은 값이면 다홍치마 잘 입어도
한미제휴 기술제휴 물건 많고 많아도
내 권리 도적 안 맞고 잘 살아도
극락일지라도

In a temple's main hall

Down with Buddha!
Down with handsome, well-fed Buddha!
What's he doing up there with that oh so casually
      elegant wispy beard?
Next, break down that painted whore of a crossbeam!
A dragon's head? What use is that, a dragon's head?
Tear down that temple, drive out the monks,
turn it all into dust and maggots!
Phaw!

Buddha with nothing, that's real Buddha!
Our foul-mouthed Seoul street-market mother,
      she's real Buddha!
We're all of us Buddhabuddhabuddha real!
Living Buddha? One single cigarette, now
there's a real cool Holy Buddha!

No, not that either.
For even supposing this world were a piece of cake,
with everyone living it up and living well,
in gorgeous high-class gear, with lots of goods produced
thanks to Korean-American technological collaboration,
each one able to live freely, with no robbing of rights,

극락일지라도
천하 없는 칠보단장 극락일지라도
사람은 날마다 이 세상 바꿔야 해요
암 그래야 하구말구
이 세상 날마다 뒤바뀌어
막 피어난 연꽃 한 송이도록 새로와야 해요
그게 부처예요

하물며 천 오백 년 머저리 달달박박 세월이야
물코 꽉 막혀 썩은 물 잠든 세월이야

Paradise, even!
Paradise, even!
utter Eden unequalled, plastered with jewels, still, even then,
day after day people would have to change the world.
Why, of course, in any case,
day after day this world must all be overturned
and renewed to become a newly blooming lotus flower.
And that is Buddha.

Down for sure with those fifteen hundred years
rolling on foolish, rumbling along:
time fast asleep like stagnant water that stinks and stinks.

인당수

우리나라에서 가장 깊은 곳이 어디냐, 인당수다.
우리나라에서 가장 깊은 사상이 어디에 있느냐.
퇴계가 아니라 몽금포의 한 극빈 처녀 심청의 결단에 있다.

성난 구름 달려라 북소리 울려라
몽구미나루 칼물결
너와바윗장 뜯어 내어라
온 세상 눈떠라
소경 아비 눈떠라
쌀 삼백 석에 몸 팔러 가거라
장산곶 한복판
수장 배 칠십 척
뱃전에 나선 시악시야
네 몸이 바람 찬 세상이어라
네 몸이 떠오른 세상이어라
네 몸이 연꽃이어라
몸 하나 뜻에 던져
남치마 푹 뒤집어 쓰고 장산곶 물에 던져
온 세상 깨달아라 싸움처럼 깨달아라
온 백성 연장 들고 달려가는 싸움이다가
그 싸움 춤이 되어
덩실덩실 춤추어라
눈떠서 새 세상이거라 심청아 심청아

Indangsu*

What is our country's deepest point? Indangsu.
Where are our country's deepest thoughts found?
Not in Toegye, the noted scholar,
but in the firm resolve of one destitute girl
from Mongkumpo, by the name of Sim-chong.

Come, clouds, driving furious!
Beat out, deep drums!
Sharp waves in Mongkum Straits,
tear away at the loose rock slabs!
Open your eyes, everyone!
Blind father, open your eyes!
Go sell yourself for sixty bushels
        of rice!
Little girl, poised on a gunwale
with seventy boats at your water burial
out there off Changsan Cape:
your body's the world with its icy winds,
your body's the world rising up again,
your body's now the lotus blossom.
One body freely tossed
with your head muffled in deep blue skirts,
tossed into the water off Changsan Cape:
awake now, world! Awake, everyone,
        like a battle!

143

After being a battle speeding,
with all our people wielding their tools,
the battle can turn into a dance
and merrily go dancing along!
Look: the world made new!
With open eyes!
Sim-chong, ah, Sim-chong, my dear!

Note ————————————————————
* In one of Korea's most famous traditional tales, the young girl Sim-
chong allows herself to be thrown into the sea at a spot called Indangsu,
in sacrifice by fishermen, in the hope of helping her blind father recover
his sight. Taken into the Dragon King's undersea palace, she is later re-
leased and found by fishermen, floating in a lotus blossom. At last, by
her daughterly virtue, her father's eyes are opened and he recognizes
her.

3

다섯 살

다섯살박이
아버지 따라 논두렁 건너오네
향기로와라
어린 가슴에 바람 안고
청룡내 잘도 건너오네
외가집 갔다 오는 길
찬 바람의 이바지 빨간 얼굴로
안성천 줄기와 갈래 만나는 일대의 넓은 세상
하늘 아래 가장 당당한 무자리 세상
어린이 세워
하늘까지 높다라이 자랑하고 싶구나
여기 있다고
여기 내일 있다고

다섯살박이
네가 곧 내일이구나
오늘의 제웅들 쓰러진 뒤
네가 백두산 상상봉의 내일이구나

다섯살박이
네 아버지
네 아버지의 아들이 아닐 때가
너에게 온다

Five years old

A five year old child trots behind his father
over the rice-field banks, the air so fragrant,
        embracing the wind,
boldly crossing the Blue Dragon Brook
after a visit to mother's folks,
a red face furnished by the biting breeze.
Look, today's vast world, there at the meeting
with Ansong Stream's meanders and torrents,
the finest of all worlds.
The child points, and I long
to boast to the clouds,
saying: Look! Here it is!
Here is tomorrow!

A five year old child!
yes, you are tomorrow, that's right!
Once today's powers-that-be have crumbled,
you are tomorrow, soaring high as Paektu Mountain.

Five year old child,
the time is coming when there will not be
a father and
a father's son;

단 하나의 아름다움이여
너로 하여금
나조차 성환 팽성까지
훤히 훤히 열린 논들을 보며 깨닫는다
반드시 둘이 아닌
한 나라를 힘껏 깨닫는다
다섯살박이
너야말로
우리가 망친 나라 일으켜서
한 나라의 어린 시절로
바람 속으로 돌아오는구나

but only the beauty of being one!
Seeing the rice fields, wide, wide stretching
as far as Pengsong and Songhwan,
even for me, awareness dawns.
Awareness dawns mighty: this nation is not two,
it is essentially one.
Five year old child, this land we have wrecked
is being raised up by you,
returning in the wind to childhood, a single land.

금남로

화순 동복 어느 마을
초상난 집에서는
사흘만에 송장 내다가 묻고
훌쩍이던 울음도 함께 묻고 돌아와
바로 그 송장 누인 방에서
산 사람은 살아갑니다
걸레질이나 한번 하면 그 방이 그냥 방입니다

몇 해만에 광주 금남로에 갔습니다
그 싸움 그 참살이 지나서
밤에는 높다라이 네온사인이 돌고
거리와 사람이 흥청대고 있었습니다
총탄 자국 때우고
언제 그런 일이 있었느냐는 듯이
자정 무렵 흰색의 도청 건물도 떠오르고 있었습니다

그러나 나는 내 창자로 꾸르륵꾸르륵 깨달았습니다
여기 와서 산 놈들 허튼 수작하지 말 것을
여기 와선 신소리 개소리 닥쳐야 할 것을

Kumnam Street

On the third day the body is duly
taken from the ancestral home
in some village up in Hwasun County
and buried, laid to rest
together with all the weeping and wailing;
on their return to the house someone alive
takes over the room where the corpse has been.
It only needs one wipe with a cloth
and the room is just a room again.

I went back to Kumnam Street in Kwangju
after several years had elapsed.
The fighting and carnage were all forgotten,
neon signs soared flashing in the evening air,
the street and the people were enjoying themselves.
The Provincial Government buildings too reared
white in the midnight gloom,
bullet-scars erased,
seeming to ask if such things had ever really happened?

But the sound of my guts rumbling told me:
No vain-glorious gestures, if you are here and alive.
No high-sounding nonsense, if you are here.

151

아르헨의 어머니

새야 새야 아르헨티나는 너무 멀구나
땅을 뚫어야 가겠구나
아르헨티나에는 새 세상이 왔단다
새 세상이란
지난 날이 하나하나 밝혀지는 세상 아니냐

아르헨티나에서는
해골 구덩이가 파헤쳐졌다
몇 만 개의 뼈들이 햇빛에 드러났다
새 세상이란 파묻은 것이 밝혀지는 세상 아니냐
사람들은 입을 다물고 뼈들이 말하는 세상 아니냐

아르헨티나의 어디에서는
어린애들의 해골 구덩이도 파헤쳐졌다
엄마 엄마 엄마 울음소리가 파헤쳐지자
새 세상 아르헨티나에 온 세상에 다시 메아리쳤다
이 세상 기막히구나 어린애가 적이 되어 처형되다니
7년 동안 병정들은 오로지 쐈다 파묻었다
어린애들이 무죄가 죄가 되어 파묻혔다

아르헨티나의 어머니들은
꺼이꺼이 살아남은 어머니들은
이제부터 제 자식의 해골을 하나하나 파내어야 한다

To the mothers of Argentina

Hey-ho! Hey-ho! Argentina's a long way away!
But bore straight down and there you are!
A new world has come in Argentina, I hear!
Now, surely a so-called new world is one
where all the things done in past days are brought to light?

They've uncovered mass graves in Argentina.
Thousands of bones have been brought to light!
Now, surely a so-called new world is one
where all the things buried are brought to light?
A world where the living shut up
and let the bones speak for themselves?

They've uncovered mass graves of children
somewhere in Argentina.
Mummy! Mummy! Mummy!
No sooner dug up, their cries echoed again
in Argentina's new world, in all the world.
What a world this is! Where kids are a threat
and have to be killed! For seven years on end
soldiers shot, then buried, shot, then buried.
Poor buried kids, their very innocence made a crime.

삽을 들고 달려가서
남편과 아들딸의 손발 잘린 시체더미를 파헤쳐서
뼈 한 개 부둥켜안고 우는 어머니에게
그 아르헨티나에 새 세상이 왔다
새 세상이란
새 세상이란
꼭 이렇게 와야 하는 것이냐

아르헨티나에는 새 세상이 왔단다
아르헨티나에는 새 세상이 왔단다

Now the mothers of Argentina,
all those mothers who barely survived, sobbing,
are anxious to dig up their children's bones.
They come rushing up, all carrying spades,
and uncover heaps of limbless corpses:
husbands, daughters, sons as well;
and to those mothers weeping,
embracing perhaps just one single bone,
to Argentina, a new world has come: a so-called new world,
a really new world! But did it have to come like that?

A new world has come to Argentina, I hear!
A new world has come to Argentina, I hear!

길

길을 보면
나에게 부랴부랴 갈 데가 있다
신영리나 내리마을을 보면
나에게 저 마을을 지나서 갈 데가 있다
그렇도다 마정리 에움길 하나에도
장호원 이백 리 길도
나에게 그냥 잠들지 못하게 한다
길을 보면
나는 불가피하게 힘이 솟는다
나는 가야 한다
나는 가야 한다
어디로 가느냐고 묻지 말아라
저 끝에서 길이 나라가 된다
그 나라에 가야 한다
한평생의 추가령지구대
그 험한 길 오가는 겨레 속에
내가 살아 있다
남북 삼천리 모든 길
나는 가야 한다
기필코 하나인 나라에 이르는 길이 있다
나는 가야 한다
나는 가야 한다

Road

Whenever I see a road, that means
I have found a place to hurry towards.
If I see a hamlet like Shinyongni or Neri,
it tells me there is somewhere beyond for me to go.
That's how it is. It only takes a by-way
in Majongni, a simple highway in Jangho-won,
and I am assured of a sleepless night.
I only have to see a road and
invariably energy comes welling up.
I must go.
I must go.
Don't ask me where I must go!
At its other end the road turns into a land.
It's to that land that I must go. You see,
I am part of this nation that has spent
its whole history on a rugged road --
the Valley Rift of Jugaryong, leading from Seoul
to the far North-east coast;
I must travel along every road
in North and South, from end to end.
For come what may there is a road

that leads to one united land.
I must go.
I must go.

햇 볕

어쩔 줄 모르겠구나
침을 삼키고
불행을 삼키자
9사상 반 평짜리 북창 감방에
고귀한 손님이 오신다
과장 순시가 아니라
저녁 무렵 한동안의 햇볕
접고 접은 딱지만하게 햇볕이 오신다
환장하겠다 첫사랑
거기에 손바닥 놓아본다
수줍은 발 벗어 발가락을 쪼인다
그러다가 엎드려
비종교적으로 마른 얼굴 대고 있으면
햇볕 조각은 덧없이 미끄러진다
쇠창살 넘어 손님은 덧없이 떠난 뒤
방안은 몇 곱으로 춥다 어둡다
육군교도소 특감은 암실이다
햇볕 없이 히히 웃었다
하루는 송장 넣은 관이었고
하루는 전혀 바다였다
용하도다 거기서 사람들 몇이 살아난 것이다

살아 있다는 것은 돛단배 하나 없는 바다이기도 하구나

Sunlight

It's absolutely inevitable!
So just take a deep breath
and accept this adversity.
But look!
A distinguished visitor deigns to visit
my tiny north-facing cell.
Not the chief making his rounds, no,
but a ray of sunlight as evening falls,
a gleam no bigger than a screwed-up stamp.
A sweetheart fit to go crazy about.
It settles there on the palm of a hand,
warms the toes of a shyly bared foot.
Then as I kneel and, undevoutly,
offer it a dry, parched face to kiss,
in a moment that scrap of sunlight slips away.
After the guest has departed through the bars,
the room feels several times colder and darker.
This military prison special cell
is a photographer's darkroom.
Without any sunlight I laughed like a fool.
One day it was a coffin holding a corpse.
One day it was altogether the sea.
A wonderful thing!

A few people survive here.

Being alive is a sea
    without a single sail in sight.

마을에 사로잡혀서

안개 개인 산 기슭
들 가운데 띄엄띄엄 그리고 둥근 포구
거기에 사람이 살고 있는 게 얼마나 환희인가
거기에 나즈막히 지붕들이 떼지어 마을을 이루어 놓은 게
얼마나 우리 모두 기막히게 좋은 일인가
마을이란 어머니보다도 어머니이다
거기가 그냥 빈 데가 아니라 마을이라는 게
얼마나 눈물겹도록 우리 모두 살 맛이 나게 하는가

지나가며 마을을 보면 어느 누구 사로잡히지 않겠는가
어느 마을에나 친척이 있다 사돈이 있다
훤한 들이나 바다까지도 사립삼고
혹은 흔한 산이라 눈 오는 날
뒷산 앞산에 포근하게 껴안긴 마을이라면
거기에서 이 시대의 참된 형제 어찌 태어나지 않겠는가
밥을 먹자 배불리 밥을 먹자
마을이야말로 개나 돼지도
우리 모두와 하나인 신뢰 그윽한 사람이게 하지 않는가

Fascinated by a human village

Look!
At the foot of mountains wrapped in mist:
houses scattered among the fields
and a curving estuary stretching beyond!
Look! people live there! what a thrill!
See how the low-set roofs come flocking together
         to form a village:
what heart-jolting joy!
A village? Our mother, more than any mother.
Not just an open space, but a village!
A thrill! What ecstasy!

Surely the sight of a village as we pass by
must fascinate everyone?
We find we have in-laws and relatives
         in every village we see.
No walls, perhaps: the open fields, even the sea
can serve as walls.
On days when snow falls on every hill
each village nestles snug
against the hillside in front or behind.
How could the truest brotherhood this age can find
         not be born there?

Let's eat, now, let's eat till we're full!
The village with all its dogs and pigs
invests each one of us with humanity
full of deep-set trust.

오늘의 썰물

우리는 기억하리라
이 세상을 폭풍우로 두들겨패야 할 때가 있다
이 세상을 성난 해일로 덮쳐야 할 때가 있다
비록 흰 거품 물고 물러서지만
오늘의 썰물로 오늘을 버리지 말자
오늘이야말로 과거와 미래의 엄연한 실재 아니냐
우리는 기억하리라
기억해 자식에게 전하리라
오 끝없는 파도의 민족이여
그러나 이 세상을 한밤중 우는 아이로 달랠 때가 있다
역사가 아버지가 아니라 내 자식일 때가 있다
오늘을 내 자식으로
멀어져 가는 썰물의 파도소리로 잠재우건만
그뿐 아니라 이 세상을 온몸으로 참회할 때가 있다
참회란 땅을 치고 후회하는 게 아니라
하지 못한 일을 끝내 해내는 데 있지 않느냐
지금 우리에게 할 일이 있다
우리는 파도치면서 젊은 밀물로 돌아오리라
우리들의 생존 몇 천 년이 오늘이 되어
바다 전체로 온누리로
우리들의 밤을 하나하나 드높은 별빛으로 기억하리라

Today's ebb tide

We shall recall.
There is a time for the world
        to be battered by storms,
a time for the world to be covered
        with raging waves.
Now white froth goes slowly drifting past
but let's not dismiss today
        with the day's ebbing tide.
Today is the stark reality
        of past and future.
We shall recall,
we shall recall, and tell our children.
Ah, nation of unending waves!
But there is a time when this world should be lulled,
        like a child that cries at midnight.
There is a time when history is not fathers but sons.
I lull today, as if it were my little child,
or the ebbing tide's distant retreating waves;
but that's not all, for a time will come
to repent whole-heartedly for what this world is.
Repenting is not a matter of beating the ground
and regretting all the mistakes of the past,
but rather, perhaps, a matter of achieving,

at last, what could not be done before?
Now we have a task to perform.
We'll all return like surging waves
borne on the youthful incoming tide.
Several thousand years of our life
have here become today,
become the whole ocean, become the whole world.
And as we all recall past nights,
each one is somehow a star up there
shining far away.

Spring after long winter

Our country folk are so tough, so strong
that even in the recent winter's bitter cold
they didn't freeze to death
but came through unscathed.
If you and I live through
a hundred such bitter winters--and now
the temperature never rises or falls,
unlike in days gone by--
we shall find we keep growing deeper,
like the winters, like the hills.
People freeze to death in the cold, of course,
but people also grow deeper by the cold.
Our folk must grow much deeper.
Why, they have to grow as deep
as Myohyang Mountain up there in the North.
In this land the monsoons
are worse than the droughts
and for those who are poor
the winter is far worse than any summer.
Someone who has never once cheated another
is already deep.
Now a few such peaceable farmers,

긴 겨울에 이어지는 봄이 우리인 것을

우리나라 사람 여싯여싯 질겨서
지난 겨울 큰 추위에도 얼어죽지 않고 무사히 보냈습니다
그러나 삼한사온 없어진 그런 겨울 백 번만 살면
너도 나도 겨울처럼 산처럼 깊어지겠습니다
추위로 사람이 얼어죽기도 하지만 사람이 추위에 깊어집
니다
우리나라 사람 좀더 깊어야 합니다
드디어 묘향산만큼 깊어야 합니다
장마 고생이 가뭄만 못하고
가난에는 겨울이 여름만 못한 것이 우리네 살림입니다
이 세상 한 번도 속여본 적 없는 사람은 이미 깊은 사람
입니다
그런 순량한 농부 하나 둘이
긴 겨울 지국총 소리 하나 없이 살다가
눈더미에 묻힌 마을에서 껌벅껌벅 눈뜨고 있습니다
깊은 사람은 하늘에 있지 않고 우리 농부입니다
아무리 이 나라 불난 집 도둑 잘되고
그 집 앞 버드나무 잘 자라도
남의 공적 가로채는 자 많을지라도
긴 겨울을 견디며 그 하루하루로 깊어서 봄이 옵니다
봄은 이윽고 긴 겨울에 이어지는 골짜기마다 우리인 것을
누가 모르랴 동네 어른이며 날짐승이며
봄이 왔다고 후다닥 덕석 벗지 않는 외양간 식구며

after long winters spent

      with never a trace of contentment or ease,

are blinking awake in snow-bound villages.

Deep folk? They're not to be found up in the sky,

      they're here among our farming folk!

Our land may be a house on fire,

thieves may prosper,

      -- willow trees tower before their homes --

and more and more people may usurp

      the good that others do,

yet still, since some endure this winter cold,

growing deeper and deeper day by day,

      in the end the spring will come.

For we are the spring, we all know that,

each one a valley leading out of long winter.

The local folk, the fluttering birds,

the beasts in the stable that don't at once

strip off their mats of straw at the news:

they all know when spring has come,

      spring busy

opening its eyes at the tip of every branch

is the bright smile already dawning

      on our faces now.

나뭇가지마다 힘껏 눈이 트는 봄이
이미 우리들의 얼굴에 오르는 환한 웃음입니다
깊은 겨울을 보낸 깊은 충만으로
우리들의 많은 할 일을 적실 빛나는 울음입니다

It is the sobbing that brightly shines
on all the many tasks that are ours now
by the fullness that comes
        from passing through deep winter.

자작나무숲으로 가서

광혜원 이월마을에서 칠현산 기슭에 이르기 전에
그만 나는 영문 모를 드넓은 자작나무 분지로 접어들었다
누군가가 가라고 내 등을 떠밀었는지 나는 뒤돌아보았다
아무도 없다 다만 눈밭에 익숙한 먼 산에 대해서
아무런 상관도 없게 자작나무숲의 벗은 몸들이
이 세상을 정직하게 한다 그렇구나 겨울나무들만이 타락
을 모른다

　슬픔에는 거짓이 없다 어찌 삶으로 울지 않은 사람이 있
겠느냐
　오래오래 우리나라 여자야말로 울음이었다 스스로 달래어
온 울음이었다
　자작나무는 저희들끼리건만 찾아든 나까지 하나가 된다
　누구나 다 여기 오지 못해도 여기에 온 것이나 다름없이
　자작나무는 오지 못한 사람 하나하나와도 함께인 양 아름
답다

　나는 나무와 나뭇가지와 깊은 하늘 속의 우듬지의 떨림을
보며
　나 자신에게도 세상에도 우쭐해서 나뭇짐 지게 무겁게 지
고 싶었다
　아니 이런 추운 곳의 적막으로 태어나는 눈엽이나
　삼거리 술집의 삶은 고기처럼 순하고 싶었다

Visit to a birch grove

Before I reached Chilhyon Mountain
on my way from Kwanghye-won one February,
somehow I found myself approaching
a broad valley thick with white birch trees.
Someone said: Go on! and gave me a shove in the back.
  I turned to see who it was.
There was no one there. But look!
How honestly the cast-off boles
  of the white birch grove confront the world!
They are altogether indifferent to the distant hills
that are fully accustomed to snow.
  The winter trees alone
know nothing of depravity.

There are no lies in sorrow. And how can anyone
  not weep at life?
In our country, for centuries
  weeping was really women's work:
weeping that would find its comfort in itself.
The birch trees live to themselves
but make me one of them.
Not everyone can come here, but it doesn't matter,

너무나 교조적인 삶이었으므로 미풍에 대해서도 사나웠으
므로

얼마만이냐 이런 곳이야말로 우리에게 십여 년 만에 강렬
한 곳이다
 강렬한 이 경건성! 이것은 나 한 사람에게가 아니라
 온 세상을 향해 말하는 것을 내 벅찬 가슴은 벌써 알고
있다
 사람들도 자기가 모든 낱낱 중의 하나임을 깨달을 때가
온다
 나는 어린 시절에 이미 늙어버렸다 여기 와서 나는 또 태
어나야 한다
 그래서 이제 나는 자작나무의 천부적인 겨울과 함께
 깨물어 먹고 싶은 어여쁨에 들떠 남의 어린 외동으로 자
라난다

 나는 광혜원으로 내려가는 길을 등지고 삭풍의 칠현산 험
한 길로 서슴없이 지향했다

the trees make themselves one with each of us;
  and they are beautiful!

As I beheld the trees, the branches of the trees,
the trembling of the tree-tops in the sky,
I grew too proud with myself and the world,
and longed to be burdened heavily,
heavily burdened with bundles of firewood.
Or rather, I longed to become gentle and mild
like a new bud born of this cold solitude; gentle and mild
as the well-cooked meat at a crossroads tavern.
Because my life was too dogmatic,
because I was harsh, even to the breeze.
How long ago was it? This kind of place?
This is that place of intensity we find
  only once in ten years.
This revered intensity!
I feel a lump rising in my throat,
my heart knows that this intensity
is not addressed to me alone,
it is addressed to the whole wide world.
The time is coming when people will realize
that they are each one part of a multitude.

When I was a child, I already grew old.
Arriving here, now I have to be born again.
So in this moment, one with the white birch's
                quite natural winter,
I return to a state of charm and prettiness,
growing up as another person's only child.

I turned my back on the road leading down
                to Kwanghyewon
and headed for the rugged mountain path leading
                towards windswept Chilhyon Mountain.

Tombstones

1

A tomb without a stone is everyone.
At such a tomb each and everyone
has a father like a mother.
A tomb without a stone
is not one single person
not one person all alone.
It's friends giving comfort
till sunset
calling the sickly beasts as well.
After death
a tomb without a stone is sacred.
It's not royal tombs that should be called sacred.
Sunny Yongin cemetery can't be called sacred.
A tomb without a stone
is no tomb at all
but everyone's warm weeping
where we all gathered, then dispersed.
It's the sleep of all, welcoming
wild geese in the evening sky.
A tomb without a stone:
so many tombs
everyone's dream.   Everyone's policy.

비 석

1

비석 없는 무덤은 만인이다
그 무덤에는
어느 누구에게도
어머니 같은 아버지가 있다
비석 없는 무덤은
단 한 사람이 아니다
단 한 사람이 아니다
병든 짐승도 불러서
해 질 때까지 달래 주는 친구들이다
죽어서
비석 없는 무덤은 거룩하다
거룩하다는 것은 왕릉이 아니다
용인땅 명당이 아니다
비석 없는 무덤은
무덤이 아니라
우리 모두 다 모였다 헤어진
만인의 따뜻한 울음이다
밤하늘 기러기 반겨 주는 만인의 잠이다
비석 없는 무덤은
수많은 무덤은
만인의 꿈이다 정치이다

2

From what I hear, there's not a headstone
        to be seen anywhere
near the remote ancestral tombs
of professor Lee Mun-yong's family.
The pride that sets up stones and things
        on tombs, that oh so natural pride,
they've quite thrown off, it seems.
The father's grave is a smallish thing,
with not a cypress in sight.
For generations now that austere family
has always practised humble ways,
spoken in humble style.
Snow has long been falling year by year
of its own modesty
and now snow is falling,
snow is falling.

2

듣자니 이문영 교수네
벽제 선산 발치엔
비석 하나 서 있지 않는다지요
무덤에 비석 따위 세우는 거만
부디부디 그 거만 내던져 버렸다지요
아버지 무덤도 자그마해서
산신나무 한 놈도 없다 하지요
그 집안의 모진 겸허 대대로 이어
말 한마디에도
언제나 저는 저는 그러지요
그러다가 그 오랜 눈 내리는 겸허로
눈이 오지요
눈이 오지요

In a radish-field

The fields of winter vegetables
 were utterly wrecked in recent storms.
Hearts greedy for water must have had a shock
at all the water in Kumoon County's paddy-fields!
The world at large won't get worked up much
 at that kind of flood disaster, though!
Levelling off the water-soaked ground,
they replanted quick-growing radish seed
 and cabbages.
While magpies, no strangers there,
 all the time kept croaking.

That's right, isn't it?
Living, then dying, is a fine thing,
but in the midst of it all
the most worthwhile task
must surely be sowing seeds?
Even if the seeds are seeds of evil;
for once that evil's grown
true men fight against it,
and as that fight extends to the ends of the earth,
that becomes the most splendid thing of all.

알타리무우밭에서

지난번 큰 비로
김장밭이 요절났다
구문리 논에서는
물 탐 많은 심뽀들 혼났겠구나
세상 물난리에 어디 이만한 일 대수랴
실컷 물 먹은 흙 다시 골라서
잘도 자라는 총각알타리무우씨도
그리고 배추씨도 새로 뿌렸다
까치들도 한 집안이라 내내 짖어댔다

안 그런가 살다가 죽는 일도 훌륭한 일이지만
그 가운데서 씨 뿌리는 일
가장 훌륭한 일 아닌가
설사 그게 악의 씨라면
그 악이 자라서
참된 사나이들이 그것과 싸우는 일은
땅 끝까지 가도록
가장 훌륭한 일이다

며칠 뒤 으시시히 추운 아침
너무나 일찍 어린 배추 싹이 돋고
알타리무우는 줄지어 불쑥 솟아 나왔다
이 얼마나 한 아름드리 기쁨이냐

A few days later, one shivery cold morning,
much too early, tiny cabbage seedlings appeared,
and rows of white radishes suddenly
        popped up their heads.
Armfuls of joy!
In our family there is nobody idle
        from early each morning
even the usual sound of humming has stopped
for each and every one has a full day
        of hard digging ahead.
Hoes, spades, rakes, sickles and such
seem like part of the family sharing rice from the pot.
The habit once properly caught and cherished,
after hoeing between the cabbage rows, today
we must weed and raise up the bone-dry ground.

Did you ever see the heavens at rest?
In all the world the most splendid thing
        most certainly is work.
And in the moments of rest between job and job
the sharing of a word or two is sweet
though there is no breath of mountain breeze.
"They say Kum-nyong's come back again?"

우리집은 이른 아침부터
누구 하나 게으르지 않고
심지어는 따라다니는 콧노래도 뭣도 두고
몸 하나 가득히 하루 하루 파헤쳐야 한다
괭이와 삽 쇠스랑 낫 이런 것도 식구인지라
한솥의 밥 먹은 것들이여
무던히도 인 박이고 소중하여
오늘은 호미질로 미호배추 솎은 뒤
이슬 마른 밭 매어 북돋아 주어야지

저 하늘이 언제 쉬는 것 보았느냐
하늘 아래 가장 훌륭한 것 그것이 일이구말구
그리고 일과 일 사이의 쉴 참에
영바람 따위 없이 나누는
몇 마디 말 얼마나 향기로우냐
금룡이네가 돌아왔다지
응 땅 파던 놈 땅 파야지
금룡이가 올해 마흔 여섯이지 아마
일 맛 알 나이지
멀리 있다가 오는 것은
하늘 아래 땅과 물에서는 훌륭한 일이다
일이 결코 기쁨인 나라
비로소 그 나라가 언젠가 우리나라 아닌가

"Of course! Once you've dug, you've got to dig."
"This year Kum-nyong must be forty-six;
that's a age to savor work."
Coming back from a long way away
is the most wonderful thing
        for earth and water.
Surely, one day ours will become a land
that finds its full joy in work.

분 꽃

분꽃은 대학 같은 건 안 다니고
10리 길 여고 나와
그냥 살림하는 처녀여요
이 미쳐 날궂이하는 세상 용케도
얌전하디 얌전한 처녀여요

진분홍 별 분꽃 흰 분꽃

어느 날 저녁
그 처녀 마당에 나와
눈에 번쩍 세상 진리 환하게
깨닫는 꽃이어요

고렷땅 어진 딸내미 순이어요 분이어요

A simple flower

This flower's not gone on to college,
nothing like that; she's a simple girl,
and after completing the local school
far down the road,
she just does the housework at home.
She's a modestly modest girl
in a crazy ill-tempered world.

The four-o'clock flower, or pride-of-Peru,
with its pink stars, and white,

is a flower that reveals
the truth about things
brightly
in the flash of an eye each day
as she comes out in the garden
early of an evening.

Simple daughters of Koryo's land:
Suni, Puni!

꽃

봄이 왔다 해도
봄이 와서 갔다 해도
웃골이나 황골 산시골에는
꽃 하나 없네
그 흔해빠진 목련도 벚꽃도 없네

다행이야 남새밭에 노란 장다리꽃 있네
이 얼마나 넘치는 기쁨이냐
산모퉁이 돌자
아 거기에 산싸리꽃 무더기 피어 있네
그러고 보니 밭 묵은 데
눈꼽 같은 냉이꽃 자욱하게 피어 있네
암 피어 있네 피어 있네

우리 산시골 꽃 구경이야 이로써 족하구말구
꽃도 쓸 만한 건 다 뽑혀 갔네
서울로 서울로
이 나라 산천에서 뽑혀 갔네

어디 꽃뿐인가
여자뿐인가
면사무소 마당 큰 나무 몇 그루
그놈들도

Flowers

Spring has come,
spring has come and gone,
and yet, up here in the mountain valleys,
there's not a single flower to be seen!
No common-or-garden magnolias,
not one cherry blossom!

Luckily in the vegetable patch
yellow flowers are blooming on a plant run to seed;
          jubilation!
Go once around the mountain, once.
Aha! Here are masses of bushes in flower!
And look there, in that field,
a carpet of tiny shepherds-purse flowers!
Here are flowers in bloom, at last!

You want to see our countryside flowers?
Well, that's it! You've seen them already.
Everything useful, even the flowers,
has all been uprooted and carried away.
Off to Seoul, off to Seoul.
All our nation's natural beauty
uprooted and carried away.

88올림픽에 어디에 뽑혀 가려고
밑둥 돌려 놓았다네

봄이 와서 갔다 해도
허허 꽃 하나 없네
텔레비젼만 있네
텔레비젼만 있네

Not only the flowers! Not only the girls!
Already the big trees in front of the village hall,
poor things,
have their roots wrapped in ropes of straw;
soon they'll be torn up and carted off too,
taken somewhere for the Olympic Games.

Spring has come and gone,
haha, and not a flower to be seen!
Only TV sets everywhere!
TV sets everywhere!

정자나무 밑

오랜 마을에는
꼭 정자나무 한 그루 계십니다
오랜 마을에서는
꼭 깊은 우물 시린 물 길어 올립니다
그 물 길어 올리는 시악씨 계십니다

점심 먹고 한동안 모이십니다
아무리 이 세상 막 되어 가도
언제나 넉넉한 정자나무 밑으로
할아범도 아범도 나오십니다
큰 나무 하나가 스무 사람 품으십니다
땀 들이고 더위 잊고
매미 쓰르라미 소리 자욱합니다
몇 마디 말 허허하고 나누십니다

가만히 보니 과연 정자나무 밑에서도
좌상 자리 있고 다음 자리 있어서
저절로 늙은이 섬기고 손윗사람 모십니다
그 무슨 개뼈다귀 예의지국이 아니라
이는 정녕 아름다움입니다 아름다운 세상입니다

Under the spreading village tree

In every old-time village
there's always one spreading village tree standing.
In every old-time village
they always draw cold water from a deep well.
And a girl always stands there
        to draw the water.

After the midday meal they meet for a while.
No matter how lawless this world becomes,
without fail the old men and women arrive,
gathering beneath the ample spreading tree.
One big tree can shelter twenty people.
Their sweat dries off, the heat is forgotten,
the chirping of the cicadas swells louder.
They share a few simple words, and laugh.

If you look carefully you will see
that even under the spreading tree
there are places of honor and other seats,
so that elders are served and shown respect.
That's no scrag-end of old-world courtesy,
it's undoubtedly beautiful
-- a world of beauty, for sure.

이 땅에 아직도 샘이 있다

제주도 바닷가에는 군데군데 샘이 있다
밀물에는 덮여버리지만
저녁 썰물에 드러나는 샘이 있다
그 물은 땅 밑으로 흘러 흘러 솟아오른다
경기도 안성땅 비산비야 문수산 고개에도
어린애같이 천진난만한 샘이 있다
꽝꽝 언 얼음 밑으로 흐르는 샘이 있다
만 년 세월아
이 땅에 아직도 샘이 있다
잘린 땅 멍든 땅
짓밟힌 땅
하늘에는 광화학스모그와 적조인데
봄가뭄 두 달인데
혁명은 30년이 되어가도 끝나지 않는데
땅은 중금속 오염으로 병들었는데
학생과 노동자 1천 5백 명이 갇혀 있는데
이 땅에 아직 샘이 있다
솟는 물 어찌 섞느냐
흐르는 물 어찌 죽느냐
그렇다
이 땅에 싸우는 사람 있다
싸우는 사람아
그대의 말은 언제나 새롭다 확신이 있다

This land still has its living springs

Here and there along the shores of Cheju Island
there are fresh water springs.
They're covered by the sea when the tide is high,
but in evening with the ebbing tide
those springs appear.
That water flows and flows underground,
    then comes gushing out.
In a valley of Mount Munsu too,
    down Ansong way,
there's a simple spring I know,
    innocent as a child;
a spring that flows from under the frozen earth.
Thousands of years of history!
This land still has its living springs.
Divided land; blasted land;
    trampled land;
though the skies are red with chemical smog,
and the springtime drought lasts a full two months,
though the Revolution's been on for thirty years
    and isn't finished yet,
though heavy metals contaminate the soil,
and fifteen hundred students and workers
    are in prison at present,

이상한지고
그대의 말에는 위선이 없다
싸우지 않는 자
싸우는 척하는 자의 위선이 없다
이상한지고
싸우다 죽어간 사람에게는 죽음이 없다
이 땅에서는 싸움이야말로 새로움이다
싸우는 때가 곧 삶이다 젊음이다
현대사가 학생항쟁사인 바 노동운동사인 바
아 솟아오르는 샘이여
흘러 흘러
천리길 땅 밑 흘러 흘러
바닷가에 솟아오르는 샘이여
삼천리 강산 언덕에서도 골짜기에서도 솟는 샘이여
흘러 흘러
저 바다에 이르는 자유여 만인의 평등이여 파도여
젊은 벗이여
이 땅에 아직도 샘이 있다
이 땅에 싸움이 있다
싸우는 사람 있는 한
뒤이어 끝나지 않는 한
이 땅은 기필코 새 세상이다
이 땅은

this land still has its living springs.
Can gushing water rot?
Can flowing water die?
Yes! This land has people who fight.
Fighters all!
Your words are perpetually new
        and full of certain assurance.
Strange to say,
your words have no hypocrisy.
None of the hypocrisy of those
        who do not fight, or only pretend to fight.
Strange to say,
those who fight until they die
        do not die.
This land can only be renewed by fight.
The hours of fight are truly life and youth.
The history of our present time
is the history of the students' struggle,
the history of the workers' movement.
Fresh gushing springs!
Flowing, flowing,
mile after mile underground,

새 나라 그 나라로
남의 나라와 함께 새 세상이다

flowing, flowing,

      then gushing out beside the sea.

Springs that gush from hillsides and valleys

all over this dear land of ours,

flowing, flowing,

and there, by the sea: Hail! freedom arising,

      equality for all, billowing waves!

Young friends!

This land still has its living springs.

This land still has its fights.

And so long as there are people who fight,

so long as all is not brought to an end,

this land can become a new world for sure!

A new nation, and as a new nation,

with other nations,

this land is indeed a new world!

5월이 가면

5월이 가면 어이하나
5월이 가면 어이하나
5월 어느 날 한밤중 계엄령이 덮쳤는데
우리는 개처럼 두들겨 맞으며 끌려갔는데
5월이 가면 어이하나
5월 어느 날 우리는 일어섰는데
천 년의 분노 움켜쥐고 맨주먹 쥐고 일어섰는데
신록의 거리 그 거리
해방의 거리 금남로에 달려가 일어섰는데
아 우리들의 가슴팍에 민주 민중 민족의 불질러
캄캄한 밤 몰아냈는데
반역의 분단
반역의 팟쇼 40년 계엄령의 탱크 앞에서 일어섰는데
노래하라 싸워라 처절히 묻어버려라 이 몸뚱아리
신록의 거리 그 거리에서
이윽고 우리는 총 맞아 쓰러졌는데
피 뿜으며
붉은 피 뿜으며 쓰러졌는데
쓰러진 송장으로 질질 끌려갔는데
횟가루 뿌려 재 뿌려
뒈진 개처럼 어디론가 실려갔는데
질주하는 군용트럭에 실려갔는데
아 망월동은 하나가 아니다 하나가 아니다

When May is gone*

What shall we do when May is gone?
What shall we do when May is gone?
One day in May at dark midnight
      martial law dropped down on us;
we were dragged away like so many dogs,
beaten and punched as we went along;
so what shall we do when May is gone?
One day in May we all rose up,
clasping a thousand years' rage in our hands,
      clenching bare fists, we all rose up.
Charging down the green-leafed road,
down Kumnam Street--Liberation Road, our road--
      we all rose up that day;
our hearts were ablaze
as we drove out dark night.
Our cry: Democracy! The Masses! The Nation!
We rose up against our land's division,
imposed betrayal,
against the tanks reinforcing
forty years' brutal martial law.
Sing! Fight! Sadly bury these bodies!
Down the green-leaved road, our road,
soon we were felled, felled by their guns,

아직도 모두 그 어딘가에
7백의총으로 8백의총으로 2천의총으로 파묻혔는데
5월이 가면 어이하나
5월 어느 날 마지막까지
도청에서 흩어져 버린 뒷골목에서
우리는 죽어간 동지의 핏자국 밟고 싸웠는데
그 이름 광주항쟁시민군으로 싸웠는데
외세와 맞서
매판과 맞서
유신잔재와 맞서
아 이 땅의 욕될 수 없는 삶을 지키다가
가슴 뚫리며 죽어갔는데
그 5월이 가면 어이하나
어느 고교생 황혼의 거리 도청 앞에서 옷을 찢으며
온 거리 떠나가라고 울부짖었는데
내 누나가 잔인무도하게 학살당했는데
나에게 총을 주세요 나도 싸울 수 있어요
그러다가 그 학생마저 총 맞아 죽어갔는데
두부처럼 짤려나간 어여쁜 너의 젖가슴
아 그렇게도 싱그러운 처녀들 임신한 아낙네 찔려서 죽어
갔는데
거리에서 골목에서 막다른 뒷골목에서
사나이들 죽어서 끌려갔는데

spouting blood, we dropped,

      spouting crimson blood.

We were dragged away, fallen corpses

covered in grey dust, covered in ashes,

we were carried away like so many dead dogs,

carried off somewhere in fast army trucks.

Ah, Mangwoldong! Not only there! Not only there!

Still they lie in unknown places,

buried there. Seven hundred? Eight hundred?

      Two thousand of us?

What shall we do when May is gone?

One day in May we fought to the end;

around the Provincial Government Capitol,

down scattered back-alleys we fought on and on,

trampling the stains of our dead comrades' blood.

We fought on, proudly bearing the name of

the Kwangju Struggle Citizens' Army.

Brought low by foreign interests,

brought low by compradors,

brought low by all the dregs of Yushin;

defending our land from further disgrace,

our breasts were pierced and so we died.

What shall we do when May is gone?

5월 어느 날 민주 민중 민족의 거리에
이윽고 야만인 그들이 닥쳤는데
양평 20사단
상무대 병력
31사단
7공수 3공수 11공수 계엄군 쳐들어와
M16소총 마구 갈겨댔는데
개머리판으로 찍어대고
총검으로 푹푹 찔러댔는데
술냄새 진하게 풍기며 투항자도 전원 사살했는데
아 그 지옥의 비명이 거리에 파도처럼 넘쳤는데
5월이 가면 어이하나
5월이 가면 어이하나
그 뒤 엄청난 공포의 도가니 무덤 같은 정적이
죽은 자와 산 자에게 길길이 뻗쳤는데
그 5월이 가면 어이하나
모든 것은 죽음으로부터 다시 시작해야 했는데
산 자들이 돌아와 통곡마저 잃어버린 그들이 돌아와
모든 것을 죽음의 거리에서 시작해야 했는데
우리는 죽어서 말이 없고
우리는 살아서 말이 없고
우리는 감옥에서 자갈 물려 바라볼 하늘도 없이
이를 악물고

As night was falling a high school boy
came tearing his clothes out there in the road
in front of the Capitol,
his shout went echoing down the street:
My sister's been murdered! It's brutal, inhuman!
Give me a gun! I can fight too!
Just then they shot him, that student died there.
A girl's sweet milky breast was sliced like curds,
        and so they sliced
gentle girls, pregnant wives, and they all died.
Down roads, down side-streets, and cul-de-sacs,
men died and were brutally hauled away.
Democracy! The Masses! The Nation!
Down that street, one day in May,
suddenly, alas, the savages drew near:
the 20th Division from Yangpyong,
        special troops,
the 31st Division,
the 7th airborne, the 3rd, the 11th,
martial law troops came smashing through.
Striking at random with M16 rifles,
smashing down butt-ends,
slashing and slashing with bayonets fixed,

가슴마다 천 년의 원한 꽉 채워서
욕된 세월 삼키고 있는데
저 능욕의 거리에서 제5공화국 군화소리 지나가는데
그 5월을 지나서 죽음을 하나씩 등에 지고
우리는 눈 내리는 날
처음으로 금남로 충장로에 나와서 눈을 맞으며
우리는 서로서로 빼앗긴 악수를 찾았는데
너 살았구나 너 살았구나 그러나
우리는 망월동으로 달려가 엉엉 울었는데
그리하여 우리는 해마다 다시 뭉쳐 일어섰는데
우리는 희미꾸레한 저쪽에 숨은 적과 원수들을
훅 훅 뜨거운 입김 불어 닦아내고 몇 번이나 확인했는데
이 땅의 하늘 높이 성조기는 펄럭대는데
이 땅은 쪽바리 득실대는데
광주는 이제 광주가 아니다 광주만이 아니다
그것은 이 땅의 역사 거점이다
그리하여 모든 거리거리마다 일어섰는데
모든 마을마다 수근거리며 모였는데
노동자의 생목숨 숯덩이가 되고
소값이 똥값 되어 농민이 농약 먹고 뻗어버렸는데
택시기사가 제 몸 불살라 쓰러지고
한 가족 몇 식구가 연탄불 먹고 식어가는데
5월이 가면 어이하나

stinking strong of drink;
all who surrendered were shot, as well.
Ah, it was hell; screaming and crying
          surging like waves.
What shall we do when May is gone?
What shall we do when May is gone?
Then over all that whirlpool of terror
spread a tomb-like silence,
covering the dead and the living alike.
What shall we do when May is gone?
We really should have started all over again
          out of death;
those who lived, forgetting to grieve,
should have started again
          out there on the streets of death;
but we have died and have no words,
we're alive and have no words,
we're in prison cooking grit,
with never a glimpse of the sky above,
we're all of us silently gnashing our teeth,
          each heart brimming full
with a thousand years' bitter resentment,
swallowing down this age of shame.

대학생이 분신자결 산화하는데
분신반 몇십 명이 줄줄이 나서고 있는데
5월이 가면 어이하나
최루탄 사과탄 개지랄탄 몇 10억 원어치로
눈에 맞아 눈 멀고 가슴 맞아 꼬꾸라지는데
돌멩이 하나 던지다가 끌려가 몰매 맞고 피 토하는데
5월이 가면 어이하나
5월이 가면 어이하나
공장에서도 학교에서도 정의의 싸움 끝나지 않고
감옥에서도 싸우고 싸워 이기는데
그러나 기만의 도시마다 혈맹의 기 끄떡없는데
일본 자민당만 삐까번쩍 드나드는데
고자 처가집 드나들 듯 드나드는데
유신 쓰레기까지 다시 돌아와 한 몫 잡는데
5월이 가면 어이하나
이 외세 이 매판 이 반역 깨부수기 위하여
이 분단과 퐛쇼 사그리사그리 쓸어내기 위하여
우리 자주와
우리 평등 우리 통일을 위하여
아 이 역사의 춤판 한바탕 춤을 위하여
오늘 처절히 썩어버려라 이 몸뚱아리
이 역사 속에 깊이깊이 묻혀서
죽어 싸우리라

The 5th Republic's army boots go clattering
            down the streets of outrage.
When that May was past, we loaded death
            on our backs,
and one bitter day for the first time went out
to Kumnam Street and Chungjang Street;
we recognized each other and retrieved
            the handshakes they had robbed us of:
You're still alive! You're still alive too!
But then we went quickly to Mangwoldong,
            and there we wept.
Since then we have united every year
            and risen up again.
Several times we have seen how
with two puffs of our hot breath
we could identify
shadowy enemies, our foes on the other side.
In our country's sky
the Stars and Stripes flies high.
Over our country, see, Japanese swarming.
Kwangju today in no longer Kwangju.
Kwangju is not just Kwangju.
It is the nucleus of our country's history.

펄펄 살아 싸우리라
우리는 이렇게 살아서 숨막히는데
5월이여
5월이여
찬란한 신록 눈부신 날의 5월이여
5월이 가면 어이하나
최루탄가스 자욱한 날
눈물 질질 흘리며
콜록대며
뻐꾸기 우는데 밤이면 접동새 슬피 우는데
5월이 가면 어이하나
아 죽어간 전사들이여 벗들이여
백 년 싸움 아직도 끝나지 않았다
백 년도 더 싸워야 한다 벗들이여
우리는 대대로 싸워야 한다
5월이 가면 어이하나
5월이 가면 어이하나
그러나 우리는 언제나 새로 뭉친다 흩어진 자 다시 모인다
피 끓어오르는 5월
온몸 퉁겨오르는 항쟁의 5월이 우리 아니냐
우리는 뭉쳐 큰 바다 파도 가르며 나아간다
5월이 가도
언제나 우리에게 5월이 살아 있다

Since then, every street has risen up.
Every village has gathered murmuring.
With workers' lives turned into lumps of coal,
with beef bought no dearer than a load of shit,
farmers have swallowed pesticide,
too many of them have fallen and died.
Taxi drivers have died in a sea of flame,
families have died by coal-brick fumes.
What shall we do when May is gone?
Students have committed self-immolation,
           a heroic end.
Dozens have volunteered,
and wait to do the same.
What shall we do when May is gone?
Billions of Won spent on tear gas bombs,
apple-shaped bombs, zig-zag bombs,
bombs have hit eyes and put them out,
bombs have hit breasts and put lives out.
You throw just one stone, you're carted off,
beaten with truncheons till you vomit blood.
What shall we do when May is gone?
What shall we do when May is gone?
In factories, in schools,

아 우리야말로 5월이다 5월이다 5월이다
온 겨레 7천만의 함성이여
그 아침 삼천리에 터져나올 환희의 전선이여 포옹이여
아 그것이 우리들의 5월이다 죽어서 이룬 해방이다
어서 오라 그 날

the fight for justice goes on unending,
in prison too, till victory comes.
But in the towns of deceit
the flag of America proudly flies.
The Japanese LDP come and go merrily.
They come and go like eunuchs
making visits to parents-in-law.
Even Yushin rubbish makes a return,
intent on grabbing its fair share too.
What shall we do when May is gone?
If we're to smash these foreign powers,
these compradors, this treachery,
if we're to sweeep away our land's division,
and this fascist rabble here,
if we're to achieve our autonomy,
our equality, our reunification,
if we're to dance for once our dance
upon old history's dance-floor here,
today we have to let our bodies
grimly rot and die.
Then, buried deep within this history,
dead, we shall fight on.
Feverishly living, we shall fight on.

217

For see how now we live suffocating.
Ah, May, May!
Glorious fresh green, dazzling days, ah May!
What shall we do when May is gone?
Days thick with tear gas,
tears pouring down,
hacking coughs,
the cuckoo is calling, in the night,
sadly, the cuckoo is calling.
What shall we do when May is gone?
Alas, dead champions, departed friends!
Our hundred year's battle is still not done!
We shall have to fight on
             a hundred years more, old friends!
We shall have to fight on from age to age!
What shall we do when May is gone?
What shall we do when May is gone?
But always we'll unite anew.
Scattered, we'll always gather again.
Blood-seething May!
Month of struggle, tossing body and soul,
May, you are us!
See us advancing united,

through the parting ocean waves!
Though May must go by,
for us May is ever alive.
Yes, we, we are May, we are May!
A great outcry arises from our people's seventy million throats.
The frontline of joy exploding that morning
in this land!
Embrace!
For such is our May! Liberation arising out of death.
May that day quickly come!

Note
* This poem portrays the violent Massacre in Kwangju in May 1980, in the course of which many were brutally killed. It evokes the ongoing dispute over the number of those who died. Mangwoldong Cemetry just outside of Kwangju holds the graves of many of the victims. The poem ends with evocations of people who took their own lives during the 1980s in protest against the dictatorial government and its policies.

커다란 봄

동부새 불어
땅 녹는다
소경눈도 뜰 만하다
아이들이
닭처럼 모인다
그러므로
땅 속 벌레도 들먹인다
저것 봐
고기들 깊은 데서
떠올라
등에 얼음 진다
어찌
하늘이 가만 있으랴
기러기아비
제 식구 데리고
송화강 간다
지금 이 나라에
커다란 일 있다
커다란 봄 하나 온다

Great springtime

Warm east winds blow,
the earth is melting.
It's a sight to open
the eyes of the blind.
Kids are clustering
close like chicks,
underground insects
are wriggling restless too.
Just look!
The fish rising
from deeper water
are using their backs
to break the ice!
How on earth
can heaven keep silent?
The wild goose fathers
are leading their broods
away towards the Sungari River.
Now in this land
wonders are happening.
One great springtime is coming!

흰 돛

그렇습니다 폭풍을 원하는 자 하나도 없습니다
그러나 저 바다 위 흰 돛이여
그대 온 심신으로 폭풍을 원하고 있습니다
폭풍 속에서만
그대 살 수 있기 때문입니다

오 껌푸른 바다 복판 인내와 갈망의 흰 돛이여
싸움이여

나 그대로부터 눈 뗄 수 없습니다

내 발 밑 풀에는
산들바람도 폭풍이거늘

A white sail

There's no one wants a gale to blow, that's sure!
And yet, white sail out there on the sea,
you yearn for a gale with all your heart;
because it's only in a gale
that you can really come alive.

One white sail of endurance and longing,
far out on the dark blue sea:
our battle!

I can't tear my eyes away.

Of course, to the grass beneath my feet,
this light mountain breeze must seem a gale!

첫 눈

첫눈 온다
이 시대 죽지 말라고
첫눈 온다
할 일 많아
산이고 물인 이 멍든 강산에
첫눈 온다

그 언제였던가
처음으로 손잡은 떨림이여 새로움이여
그 첫사랑으로
빈 나뭇가지마다
빛나던 이름이여
이제 그 이름 아득한 거리에
첫눈 온다

돌이킬 수 없이 내 순결과 오욕 헐헐 바쳐
여기까지 이르렀건만
결코 사랑일 수 없는 미움으로
원수를 원수라 부를 자유도 없는 미움으로
이 시대가 무엇이더냐
여기저기 숨어 있다가
끝내 부릅뜬 눈 감고 붙잡혀 가는 젊은것이여
너에게

First snow

The first snow is falling, and
tells this generation not to die!
The first snow is falling!
On our dear land of water and hills
--harshly bruised, true--
the first snow is falling!
So much to be done!

How many years has it been, I wonder?
The trembling newness of first holding hands,
a name that shone on every empty branch
by the power of love's first flame.
Now the first snow is falling
in streets where that name is quite unknown!

There's no going back in life, after coming so far
offering my innocence and my disgrace,
　　　without regret;
but what has this generation come to?
By a hatred that can never be love,
by a hatred that has not even the freedom
to call a foe a foe.
The first snow is falling on you,

첫눈 온다
잡아가는 것이여
너에게도 온다

처절히 이 시대 막바지 바라보노니
온 마음 뜨겁게 뭉쳐 흩어질 줄 모르는 것이여
흩어졌다가
또다시 모이는 것이여
그 누구 있어
이 강산 잘린 허리 등져 버리느냐
갇힌 누이 시퍼런 노래 퍼지는 지붕에
모든 지붕에
모든 바다 너머너머 달려와 깨지는 파도 위에
싸움 위에
첫눈 온다
이 시대 죽지 말라고
이 강산
온통 숨쉬라고 온다
개 같은 슬픔도 슬픔일진대

young friends arrested, hauled away,
your angry eyes closed at last,
after hiding here and there a while,
And on you who hauled them away
it's falling, too!

Such grief to see this generation's last days!
Yet see that unity of burning hearts,
so strong it cannot be broken!
And if ever it's broken, coming together again!
Can there be any who will turn their backs
and ignore the division at the waist of our lovely land?
The first snow is falling
on the prison roof over which
my sisters' sharp-edged songs once spread,
and every roof
and on the waves of every sea
that come rolling shorewards too too fast
and break
and on our battle.
It's falling to tell this generation
not to die!
To tell our land of rivers and hills:

Take breath again!
Cursed grief is also grief, you know.

Dream poem

Something personal.

Sometimes I have written poems in my dreams.
From the time when I was twenty or thirty
until now
a good number of poems written in dreams
lie there, useless.

Because what I write in my dreams
is all forgotten once I wake up, you see.

Then too there are phrases,
not in dreams,
that come to me on waking in the night,
splendid phrases;
next morning, though,
they're all forgotten.

You
phrases that just brush past me,
and never come back!

꿈 시

내 이야기 하나

나는 이따금 꿈속에서 시를 쓴다
스무 살 서른 살 이래
이제가지 꿈속에서 쓴 것
몇 편
놀고 있다

꿈속에서 쓴 것
깨어나 몽땅 잊어버리기도 한다

꿈 아니라
한밤중 잠 깨어
떠오른 구절
빛난 구절
그러나 아침이면 잊어버리기도 한다

나에게 스쳐 갔을 뿐
다시 오지 않는 구절
그대

뒷날 내 삶의 부스러기 있어
집도 없이 떠돌다가

Some day some scraps of my life
roaming around,
with no home of their own
may enter a stranger's village.
Then bounding away after entering there,
will they head for some cosmic space?
Nine hundred light years away?
Nine hundred light years or more?

Yes! Phrases that came to me and left:
you are never destined to become a poem;
you are orphans in outer space
with neither life nor tomb.

어느 누구의 낯선 마을에 들어갈 것인가
들어가자마자 뛰쳐나와
어느 우주로 갈 것인가
9백 광년이나
9백 광년 이상이나

그렇다 나에게 왔다 간 구절
그 구절구절이야말로
끝끝내
시가 되어서는 안될 우주의 고아이다
삶도 무덤도 없는

열매 몇 개

지난 여름내
땡볕 불볕 놀아 밤에는 어둠 놀아
여기 새빨간 찔레열매 몇 개 이룩함이여

옳거니! 새벽까지 시린 귀뚜라미 울음소리
들으며 여물었나니

아침이슬

여기 어이할 수 없는 황홀!
아아 끝끝내 아침이슬 한방울로 돌아가야 할
내 욕망이여

Fruit

Last summer's
efforts of the blazing burning sun
the efforts of the dark by night
have brought into being
these few bright crimson hips on a dog-rose briar.

Which is as it should be: they ripened to the sound
of the chilling nightlong cricket's song.

Morning dew

Ecstasy without words:
my craving must in the end revert
to being a single drop of morning dew!

눈 내리는 날

눈 내린다
마을에서 개가 되고 싶다
마을 보리밭에서 개가 되고 싶다
아냐
깊은 산중
아무것도 모르고
잠든 곰이 되고 싶다
눈 내린다
눈 내린다

Snowfall

Snow is falling.
I want to become a village dog
I want to become a dog
out in the village barley fields.
No
I want to become a bear
asleep, aware of nothing,
deep in the hills.
Snow is falling.
Snow is falling.

추운 날

추운 날
춥고 바람 부는 날
아 거기 살고 싶어라
결코 따뜻한 것만이 복되지 않다
추운 날
떨어진 나뭇잎새
다 구을러 가버린 추운 날
으시시히
몸 움츠러들며
아 거기 살고 싶어라

집집마다 김장 끝나
그 김치 익어 가며
아 거기 살고 싶어라

에움길 마구 달리는 개 보아라
소리치는 아이들 보아라
바람에 휘어지는
빈 현사시나무 우듬지 까치 보아라
아 거기 살고 싶어라

아 춥고 바람 부는 날 기뻐라
하늘 아래 가득히 기뻐라

A cold day

A cold day
A cold and windy day
How I long to live there
Warmth is not the only happiness
A cold day
A cold day when all the fallen leaves
go rolling spinning away
Brrrrrrr
Shivering
How I long to live there

Every house has made its winter kimchi
and now that kimchi's ripening
How I long to live there

See that dog racing blindly
down the winding trail
See those children shouting
See the magpies perched at the tip
of that aspen bending in the wind
How I long to live there

Rejoice, cold and windy day
Rejoice most fully, here beneath the sky

새 싹

씨 뿌렸더니
여기
여기
저기 좀 보소

어제는 누가 흙으로 돌아가더니
오늘 아침 이렇게 태어나
이 세상 만년 파릇파릇 새싹이구려

결국 여기서는
나에게까지
나에게까지
급한 물에 떠내려온 나에게까지
곡식 익은 뒤의 추위 가운데
사랑밖에 없다

저기 저기 좀 보소

Fresh buds

I sprinkled seeds
here
here
Look at that!

Yesterday someone returned to clay
and this morning that person is reborn
like this, so
the ancient world is springing
fresh and green

Here at last
even I
even I
even I washed drifting down
on rapid streams
am utter love
in the chill that follows harvest-time

Look! Look at that!

호박꽃

그동안 시인 33년 동안
나는 아름다움을 규정해왔다
그때마다 나는 서슴지 않고
이것은 아름다움이다
이것은 아름다움의 반역이다라고 규정해왔다
몇 개의 미학에 열중했다
그러나 아름다움이란
바로 그 미학 속에 있지 않았다
불을 끄지 않은 채
나는 잠들었다

아 내 지난날에 대한 공포여
나는 오늘부터
결코 아름다움을 규정하지 않을 것이다
규정하다니
규정하다니

아름다움을 어떻게 규정한단 말인가
긴 장마 때문에
호박넝쿨에 호박꽃이 피지 않았다
장마 뒤
너무나 늦게 호박꽃이 피어
그 안에 벌이 들어가 떨고 있고

Pumpkin flower

For thirty-three years as a poet
I merrily defined what beauty was.
Each time, without hesitation
I would declare: beauty is like this, or:
this is a betrayal of beauty.
I went crazy over several different kinds
of aesthetic theory.
But beauty was never
in those aesthetic theories.
I was falling asleep
with the light on.

What fear in the days gone by!
From now on I will strictly refrain
from any definitions of beauty!
Define away!
Define away!

As if beauty can ever be defined!

All through the weeks of summer rain
no flowers bloomed on the pumpkin creepers.
Now the rains are over

그 밖에서 내가 떨고 있었다

아 삶으로 가득찬 호박꽃이여 아름다움이여

and at long long last a flower has bloomed,
inside it a bee is quivering,
outside it I am quivering.

Pumpkin flower brimming full of life:
you are true beauty!

김신묵

아흔여섯 살 김신묵은
내가 죽으면 박수치며 보내달라 하고 죽었다
장례식날
그의 관이 나갈 때
박수를 쳤다
그 누구도 박수치지 않는 자 없다
산에다 묻어버리고 내려올 때
그의 말이 들렸다
박수치며 내려가라고
그래서 하나둘 박수를 쳤다

동두천 의정부 사이의 길이 양키 없이 빛났다

Kim Shin-muk*

At ninety-six, Kim Shin-muk
said: When I die,
see me off with applause!
Then she died.
The day of the funeral
as her coffin was carried out
we all clapped,
everyone without exception clapped.
Coming down from the hills
after burying her there
we recalled her words:
Go back down clapping.
So a few people clapped.

The road between Tongduchon and Uijongbu
stretched glorious, not a Yank in sight!

Note ───
* Kim Shin-muk was the mother of the dissident pastor Moon Ik-hwan.

간 첩

여보게 자네 간첩의 고독을 아는가
아무에게도 그 자신을 숨겨야 하는 그 고독을 아는가
아무에게도 그 자신을 숨길 뿐 아니라
그에게 부과된 조국을
아무에게도 말할 수 없는 고독을 아는가
그러다가 모르츠 부호의 거점에게 체포되어
사형에서
무기형으로 감형
20년 이상을 0.7평짜리 마루에서
흰 머리로 덮인
그 길고 긴 나날의 고독을 아는가

더욱 놀라운 것은
그들은 20년 전의 신념 그대로인 고독이라네
시대 흘러
그 신념이 티끌이 되고 마는데도
그 고독으로부터 손을 펼 줄 모른다네
아 무엇이 비석이고 무엇이 바람 한 점이란 말인가

Spies

Hey! Do you realize what loneliness
a spy has to endure?
Do you realize the loneliness involved
in hiding yourself from everyone?
And not only in hiding from everyone;
do you realize the loneliness involved
in not being able to tell a soul
about the country you are engaged to serve?
Then, arrested for morse-code communications,
condemned to death,
commuted to life imprisonment,
do you realize the long loneliness involved
in spending more than twenty years,
the long long loneliness day after day,
in a cramped cell with a wooden floor
and your hair already white?

Even more surprising, though, is the fact
that their loneliness is the fervor
of twenty years ago!
Although as time passed
that fervor all turned to dust,
they cannot let go

of that loneliness!
I ask you: which shall we call a tombstone,
and which a breath of air?

그대의 웅변

나는 그대가 강연할 때마다
그 웅변이
젊은이들을 압도할 때마다
그곳을 박차고 일어난다
그대의 웅변에는 확신뿐이니까
머리카락 한 개의 고뇌도 없으니까
아냐
그대의 웅변에는 진짜 확신이 없으니까

나는 그대를 경멸하기 이전에
그대의 웅변에 놀아나는 사람들을 경멸한다
푸른 하늘 대신

Your eloquence

Every time you make a speech,
every time your eloquence
is about to overwhelm your young hearers,
I get up and get out.
Because in your eloquence
there is utter assurance,
and not one hair of torment?
No!
Because in your eloquence
there is no true assurance at all.

Before I despise you, I despise
all those who go wild at your words.
On behalf of the heavens above.

경허스님

경허는 숫제 머리를 길러버렸다
옷도 바꿔버렸다
법호도 바꿔버렸다
경허로부터
난주로 바꿔버렸다
다 버리고
삼수갑산으로 들어갔다
시시한 마누라도 얻어
서당 훈장노릇 했다
그러다가 거기서 죽었다
내일 떠나네 하고

쯔쯔 내일 떠나네 그 소리가 군더더기라

The monk Kyong-ho

Kyong-ho let his hair grow long.
He put on different clothes.
He gave up his Buddhist name.
From being called Kyong-ho
he took the name Nan-ju.
He gave up everything he had
and went into seclusion.
He got himself a plain wife,
and a job as a village teacher.
And he died there,
saying: I'll leave tomorrow.

Tut tut! No need to say I'll leave tomorrow.

외할머니

소 눈
멀뚱멀뚱한 눈
외할머니 눈

나에게 가장 거룩한 사람은 외할머니이외다

햇풀 뜯다가 말고
서 있는 소

아 그 사람은 끝끝내 나의 외할머니가 아니외다
이 세상 평화외다

죽어서 무덤도 없는

Grandmother

Cow eyes
those dull vacant eyes
my grandmother's eyes.

My grandmother!
The most sacred person in the world to me.

A cow that has stopped grazing the fresh grass
and is just standing there.

But that's not my grandmother after all!
It's this world's peace,

dead and denied a tomb.

대보름날

정월 대보름날 단단히 추운 날
식전부터 바쁜 아낙네
밥손님 올 줄 알고
미리 오곡밥
질경이나물 한 가지
사립짝 언저리 확 위에 내다 놓는다
이윽고 환갑 거지 회오리처럼 나타나
한바탕 타령 늘어놓으려 하다가
오곡밥 넣어가지고 그냥 간다
삼백예순 날 오늘만 하여라 동냥자루 불룩하구나
한바퀴 썩 돌고 동구 밖 나가는 판에
다른 거지 만나니
그네들끼리 무던히도 반갑구나
이 동네 갈 것 없네 다 돌았네
자 우리도 개보름 쇠세 하더니
마른 삭정이 꺾어다 불 놓고
그 불에 몸 녹이며
이 집 저 집 밥덩어리 꺼내 먹으며
두 거지 밥 한 입 가득히 웃다가 목메인다
어느새 까치 동무들 알고 와서 그 부근 얼쩡댄다

New Year's Full Moon

Bitter cold day, the new year's first full moon,
a special day.
One housewife, busy from early morning,
knowing that beggars will be coming by,
puts out a pot of five-grain rice in anticipation
on the stone mortar
that stands beside her brush-wood gate,
with a single side-dish of plantain-shoots.
Soon, an ancient beggar comes breezing up,
makes ready to spin a yarn but finally
just pockets the rice and goes on his way.
If only we had 360 more days like today in a year!
His bag is soon bulging.
As he is leaving the village, his turn made,
he runs into another beggar:
glad encounter!
You've no call to go there, I've done'em all!
Let's us celebrate a Fool Moon too!
Snapping dried twigs, they make a fire
to thaw themselves by, then
producing hunks of rice from this house and that,
the two beggars set to,
choking, laughing with mouths full.

Soon bands of magpies hear the news
and flock flapping around.

Old Foster-father

See that migrant lapwing perching on a branch!
There was an old man used to say
     birds weren't strangers either;
even when he was upset
he would never go on bitterly complaining,
although his cuffs were caked with dirt.
And his sons, the apples of his eye,
he lost them both:
one died of cholera,
the other fell into the water and drowned.
He could barely sigh; he had nothing to live for.
Then, once past forty,
he began collecting foster children,
     one after another;
there was one was about ten years old,
another who had lost both parents early on,
he took them all into his house,
made them his own,
     then sent them out at the proper time.
When harvest festival season came
unkind neighbors used to make sly remarks
about why does a man need so many foster children?
While to each the old man would dole out a measure

수양영감

철새 댕기물새 가지에 앉는다
새도 남이 아니라고 말하는 영감
비롯 옷소매 땟국은 잘잘 흐를지라도
노여울 때도 쓸스레 그냥 넘긴다
제 아들
깻묵 같은 아들 둘 잃고 나서
하나는 호열자로
하나는 물에 빠져 죽어서
이 세상 살 생각 통 없다가 한숨도 못 쉬다가
마흔 살 넘어
여남은 살쯤 되는 아이
조실부모 아이
이놈 저놈 수양아들 삼았다
집에 두기도 하고
다 친자식 만들어 사정 따라 보내기도 하고
추석 무렵 다가오면
햇대추 후려쳐 한 됫박씩 손수 가져다주는 영감
동네 사람들 괜히 비아냥거리기를
웬놈의 수양아들 그리도 많이 두노
그러나 그 영감 차락차락 가라앉은 소리로
사람이 귀한 줄 알면 다 부모 같고 자식 같지 않은가
그 영감 중뜸 비알밭 콩밭두렁 풀 깎다가
산등성이 쭈뼛이 오르는 바람에

of fresh jujubes he had beaten from the tree
and simply answer in a quiet level voice:
If only you realized how precious people are!
Isn't each person like a parent or a child?
And when that old man had done weeding
between the rows in his hillside bean-patch,
as he watched how the sluggish uphill-climbing breeze
overturned the bean-leaves with a flash of white,
he would mutter: Here, it's that rogue's birthday tomorrow,
better pop a middling hen in a bag presently
and call in there on the way back home;
he's a growing lad: not good if he's hungry,

      not good at all.

일제히 뒤집어진 하얀 콩잎 돌아보더니
참 내일이 그놈 생일이지
이따가 중병아리 한 놈
구럭에 넣어 다녀와야지
크는 놈이라 속이 허하면 안되지 안되구말구

No-more's mother

Three daughters had already been born
to No-more's parents over in Kalmoi:
Toksuni
Boksuni
Kilsuni.
Then another daughter emerged; once again
the sacred straw stretched across the gate
held bits of charcoal, but no red peppers!
She got the name No-more.
Furious, No-more's father went drinking;
when he came home, he declared:
A woman that can only have girls
deserves to be kicked out of the house!
He grabbed his wife by the hair,
although she had not yet fully recovered,
and dragged her outside,
smashing down the rotten fence.
Uhuhuh, he cried. A fine sight.
But oh the tasty red-pepper paste
that No-more's mother makes!
How ever does she do it? Why, people come
from Namwon, and even from Sunch'ang,
eager to learn her pepper-paste art.

딸그마니네

갈뫼 딸그마니네집
딸 셋 낳고
덕순이
복순이
길순이 셋 낳고
이번에도 숯덩이만 달린 딸이라
이놈 이름은 딸그마니가 되었구나
딸그마니 아버지 횟술 먹고 와서
딸만 낳는 년 내쫓아야 한다고
산후 조리도 못한 마누라 머리 끄덩이 휘어잡고 나가다가
삭은 울바자 다 쓰러뜨리고 나서야
엉엉엉 우는구나 장관이구나
그러나 딸그마니네 집 고추장맛 하나
어찌 그리 기막히게 단지
남원 순창에서도 고추장 담는 법 배우러 온다지
그 집 알뜰살뜰 장독대
고추장독 뚜껑에
늦가을 하늘 채우던 고추잠자리
그 중의 두서너 마리 따로 와서 앉아 있네
그 집 고추장은 고추잠자리하고
딸그마니 어머니하고 함께 담는다고
동네 아낙들 물 길러 와서 입맛 다시며 주고받네
그러던 어느 날 뒤안 대밭으로 순철이 어머니 몰래 들어가

A few of the host of pepper-red dragonflies
that fill the clear late-autumn skies
often come down and perch on the heavy lids
of the bulging pots of red-pepper paste
up on the frugal storage platform
there behind the house;
the local women at the well,
with much smacking of lips, claim
that special pepper paste is made
by No-more's mother and the red dragonflies,
working in collaboration!
On one such day, Sunch'ol's ma came sneaking
into the bamboo-fenced back yard
to scoop out one bowl of the famous paste,
and as she did so, the daughter called Toksuni
happened to be there washing her back.
Struck by the sight of that abundant flesh
she murmured:
My! Sunch'ol dear, it's Toksuni here
that you should marry! A hometown bride!
I never saw such a luscious girl!

그 집 고추장 한 대접 떠가다가
목물하는 그 집 딸 덕순이 육덕에 탄복하여
아이고 순철아 너 동네장가로 덕순이 데려다 살아라
세상에는 그런 년 흐벅진 년 처음 보았구나

The women from Sonjae

In darkest night, near midnight, the dogs
in the middle of Saeto start to bark raucously.
One dog barks so the next one barks
until the dogs at Kalmoi across the fields
follow suit and start to bark as well.
Between the sounds the barking dogs produce
echo scraps of voices: eh ah oh…
Not unrelated to the sound the night's wild geese
let fall to the bitter cold ground
as they fly past high above,
not unrelated to that backwards and forwards
echoing splendid sound.
It's the women from Sonjae on their way home
from the old-style market over at Kunsan
where they went with garlic bulbs by the hundred
borne in baskets on their heads,
since there's a lack of kimchi cabbages
from the bean-fields;
now they're on their way home, after getting rid
of what couldn't be sold
at the knock-down auction at closing time;
several miles gone
several left to go in deepest night!

선제리 아낙네들

먹밤중 한밤중 새터 중뜸 개들이 시끌짝하게 짖어댄다
이 개 짖으니 저 개도 짖어
들 건너 갈뫼 개까지 덩달아 짖어댄다
이런 개 짖는 소리 사이로
언뜻언뜻 까 여 다 여 따위 말끝이 들린다
밤 기러기 드높게 날며
추운 땅으로 떨어뜨리는 소리하고 남이 아니다
앞서거니 뒤서거니 의좋은 그 소리하고 남이 아니다
콩밭 김치거리
아쉬울 때 마늘 한 접 이고 가서
군산 묵은 장 가서 팔고 오는 선제리 아낙네들
팔다 못해 파장떨이로 넘기고 오는 아낙네들
시오릿길 한밤중이니
십리길 더 가야지
빈 광주리야 가볍지만
빈 배 요기도 못하고 오죽이나 가벼울까
그래도 이 고생 혼자 하는 게 아니라
못난 백성
못난 아낙네 끼리끼리 나누는 고생이라
얼마나 의좋은 한 세상이더냐
그들의 말소리에 익숙한지
어느새 개 짖는 소리 뜸해지고
밤은 내가 밤이다 하고 말하려는 듯 어둠이 눈을 멀뚱거린다

The empty baskets may be light enough
but empty-stomached with nothing to eat,
I wonder just how light they feel?
Still, they don't each one suffer on her own.
It's a pain they share,
these plain simple people
these plain simple women.
What a good homely life!
Perhaps the dogs have got used to their voices,
for the barking starts to die away,
night seems eager to declare: I myself am night!
And the darkness blinks its vacant eyes.

병옥이

두메 촌놈으로 태어나면
대여섯 살에 벌써
노는 놈 없다
산같이 쌓인 일에 아버지 따라 일꾼 되어야 한다
가을 오면
우렁 잡아오라는 어머니 말 듣고
논으로 달려가
드넓은 논바닥
우렁 뒤지는 한나절 좋다 참 좋다
그놈의 일구더기 떠나서 좋다
병옥이
우렁 잘 잡는 병옥이
양잿물 잘못 먹고 죽어버렸다
동네 아이들 병옥이 무덤 아무도 몰랐다
아이들 죽어야 무덤도 없다 제사도 없다 또 낳는다

Pyongok

If you're born a yokel out in the backwoods,
once you've reached five or six
there's no time left for play,
you're forced to become a drudge
following your father,
with work piling up like the hills.
When autumn comes,
if mother tells you to bring home mud-snails
you go rushing out to the rice-paddy:
foraging for snails half a day
in the wide open spaces out there
is great, really great.
Being away from his rotten jobs is great.
Pyongok,
expert snail-catcher Pyongok,
drank lye by mistake and died.
None of the neighborhood kids knew
where he was buried.
If a kid dies there's no tomb, no offerings,
there'll be another one born by-and-by.

봉 태

나하고 국민학교 일이등 다투었지
부자집 아들이라
옷이 좋았지
항상 단추 다섯 빛났지
도시락에 삶은 달걀 환하게 들어 있었지
흰쌀밥에 보리 뿌려졌지
그러나 누구한테 손톱발톱만치도 뽐낸 적 없지
너희 논 옆에 우리 논 하나 있다
너하고 나도
의좋게 지내자고 굳은 떡 주며 말했지
그런 봉태
수복 직후 아버지 죽은 뒤
동네사람에게 끌려가서
할미산 굴 속에서 죽었지
유엔군 흑인 총 맞아 죽었지
그 달밤에
그 캄캄한 굴 속에서 죽었지
봉태야
나는 너 하나 살려낼 수 없었다
네 열일곱 살은 내 열일곱 살이었는데

Pongtae

You and I vied for first place in grade-school.
You were from a rich house
had really nice clothes
your five buttons were always shining bright and
every day a boiled egg snuggled
bright in your lunch-box where the white rice
was only sprinkled with barley;
but you were never boastful, oh no,
not by so much as a finger-paring.
We had a paddy-field just beside yours.
Let's you and I get on well together,
you said, and gave me dried rice-cakes.
But Pongtae,
first your father died
when the Reds pulled back north,
then you were dragged off by the local people;
you died in a cave in Halmi Mountain,
you died shot by a black UN soldier.
One moonlit night
in a dark cave you died.
Pongtae, ah, I could do nothing to save you,
though you were sixteen
and I was sixteen.

재숙이

시암안집 처녀 재숙이
찰찰 넘치는 물동이 이고 가며
먼데 바라보기도 한다
첫가을 백리가 탁 트였구나
내년에는
우리 동네 떠날 재숙이
온통 부푼 재숙이
달 진 뒤의 어둠 같은 재숙이

Chaesuk

Chaesuk from the house by the well,
a brimming crock of water perched on her head,
gazes into the far-off distance
    as she walks along:
the early autumn open road lies clear ahead.
Next year
Chaesuk will be leaving here.
Chaesuk's heart swells in expectation.
Chaesuk, so like the darkness left
    after the moon's gone down!

우 물

그 집 안에는 우물이 있어요
열 길도 넘는 우물이 있어요
그윽한 분례네 집
분례 어머니 박꽃처럼 환한 분례 어머니하고
어린 분례하고 옥잠화하고
단 두 식구 살고 있어요
젊은 과수댁이라
말 한 마디도 삼가고
한여름 등물도 한 적 없어요
그 분례 어머니가
열 길 우물에 묵직한 두레박 내려뜨려
길어올린 검푸른 물
그 물의 고요와 그 무서움
심부름 가서
한 모금 마시고 나면 온몸 떨려요 두근두근대어요

The well

There's a well beside that house.
A well more than ten fathoms deep,
there beside Pollye's snug family house.
Pollye's mother, bright as a gourd-flower,
and little Pollye, a lily-flower,
just the two of them live there together.
The mother a widow, young,
discreet in every word,
never dousing herself with water,
       even in midsummer heat.
When I used to go on errands there,
if I took one sip of the blue-black water,
of that water's silence and the dread
that Pollye's mother,
       letting down the heavy bucket,
drew up from her ten-fathom well,
my whole body would tremble, my heart would pound.

쌍동이 어머니

병현이 병진이 쌍동이 어머니
축 늘어진 젖 드러내놓고
사방팔방 휘저어 다니는 아낙네
태풍에 칙간 무너진 뒤
동네 남정네 보건 말건
수숫대 서걱이는 밭에
궁둥이 까고 오줌 뿜는 아낙네
반찬 없으면
남의 집 푸성귀도 마구 뜯어다가 삶는 아낙네
쌍동이 가운데 한 놈이
동네 아이들과 놀다가 맞아 울고 오면
저런 오사급살할 놈! 벼락 맞아 뒈질 놈!
아니 삼복더위에 생짚 깔고 퍼질러놓으니
남한테 얻어맞고나 다니다니
이렇게 막된 쌍동이 어머니
이런 아낙네한테도
지난 날 부끄러워하고 수줍은 처녀시절이 있었을 터
얼마나 얼마나 귀한 시절일 터

The twins' mother

Pyonghyon and Pyongjin's mother?
See her bare her dangling breasts
and go rushing around in all directions.
After the monsoons have demolished the outhouse,
not caring if the menfolk see or not,
she bares her bottom in the millet-crunchy fields
and pisses freely. That kind of woman.
If there's nothing to eat at home,
she grubs up a neighbor's greens to cook.
What a woman!
If one of the twins
comes running home screaming
from being punched playing with the local kids:
A plague on you! Lightning strike you dead!
No one would think you were born
on fresh straw one midsummer dog-day!
How come you get beaten up all the time?
That's how wild the twins' mother is
and yet even such a woman must once have known
shy modest days of maidenhood,
those precious days!

283

앵두꽃

새터 오목이네 집
초가삼간인데
얌전하디 얌전한 집
쌀 보리 밀 콩 팥 옥수수 수수 차조 귀리
무엇 하나 없는 것 없다
다섯곡식 일곱곡식 없는 것 없다
우리 동네 알뜰한 집
오목이 어머니
그 아금발이 살림솜씨
늘 낭자 곱고
앞치마 푼 적 없다
키질하면
들깨알 하나 조낱 하나 까불어 나가는 법 없다
그 집에
긴 겨울 가
봄이 오면
앵두나무 두 그루
앵두꽃 피어
다 일 나가고 빈집인데
그 집 가득히 빛내주고 있다
환하게 빛내고 있다
어이쿠 원통해라
어느 복 터진 잡놈 있어

Plum blossom

The house down Bird Lane where Omok lives
is only a tiny thatched cottage and yet
so spick and span,
lacking in nothing, be it
rice barley wheat soy-beans red-beans maize
sorghum millet and oats as well,
all the five or seven kinds of grain and corn,
all there:
the most frugal household around.
Omok's mother:
such a careful housekeeper
with her hair tidy in a bun,
her apron never off.
When she winnows the rice
not one stray seed, sesame or millet,
escapes from the tossing.
In that house,
when winter is gone
and spring returns,
two plum-blossom trees
stand blooming,
so that although the house is empty
when the two are out working,

그 집으로 장가 들어
오목이 어머니 빼다박은 오목이 업어갈지
업어가다가 발병 날지

those trees make the house all brightness.
But alas, lament the pity of it!
One fine day or other some lucky fellow
will come marrying there
and carry off Omok, so like her mother,
he'll carry her off on his back,
on his back; I hope he gets sore feet.

똘

똘에 가보아라
똘물 정답다
할머니 같다
어려운 몇 고비 넘긴
아주머니 같다
거짓말이다
멀리 가사메까지 이어진 똘에
들심부름 갔다오다가
똘에 빠져 죽은
재남이네 계집아이
이름도 없고
부모도 없는 아이
때와 곳 주인 눈이라
어디 울 곳 있나
제대로 울어보지도 못한 아이
똘에 가보아라
그 아이 같다
그 아이 죽인 물이
그 아이 같다

The ditch

Go and look in the ditch.
How friendly the water there is:
like an old lady.
Like a matronly lady
who has weathered a fair number of hardships.
All lies!
Chaenam's little maid,
running errands to that far-off ditch,
fell in and drowned.
A child without a name,
without parents.
All the time everywhere her master's eye watching,
she had no place to cry alone,
that child could never cry properly.
Go and look in the ditch.
It's like that child.
The water that drowned that child
is like that child.

이년아

새소리 나기 전부터
손에 일 들고
한밤중 거지별 기울어서야
일 놓아도
집안일이란 빛도 끝도 없다
밭일이나
논일이야 뚝딱 끝이 있건만
한규 할아버지 소실댁네 계집아이
빛도 끝도 없다
가뜩이나 밥상 많이 차리는 집
술상 내는 집
벌써 재작년인가
여섯번째로 들어온 계집아이
굶어 쭉 뻗는 부황철에
삼시 세때 남은 밥덩이라도 그게 어디냐
그저 이년아 하면
예 하고 뒤안에서 일하다가도
앞마당으로 뛰어오고
우물가 양잿물 빨래 헹구다가도
제 몸보다 큰 빨래 짜다가도
이년아
이년아 하면
예 하고

Hey, you there!

Setting to work long before the dawn chorus begins,
and only stopping at midnight
when the evening star is setting:
housework knows no glory, no end.
Field-work, now, or paddyfield-work,
one, two, they have an end,
but for old Hankyu's concubine's maid
there's no glory, no end.
A house with mountains of meals to prepare,
and tables of drinks to serve.
Just look at that girl, the sixth to go there:
can it already be two years ago?
It was the year of the great famine
so she thought herself lucky
to survive on scraps left-over from meals.
If she hears a call: Hey, you there!
even though she's working round at the back,
she replies: Right away!
and comes running out to the yard in front;
or maybe she's beside the pump, rinsing the washing in lye,
or wringing out a pile of clothes
rather bigger than herself, but
if she hears a call: Hey, you there!

큰방 마나님한테 달려간다
동네 아낙이
어쩌다가
너 그 집 1년 있다가는 뼈도 못 추린다
다른 집 가서
밥 얻어먹고 살아라
골병든다
이런 소리 들어도
한 귀에서 한 귀로 빠져나가고
천근 같은 두레박줄 우물에 내리며
하마터면 두레박줄하고
함께 내려갈 뻔하였구나
이년아
이년아

she replies: Right away!
and hurries to where her mistress is.
From time to time local women say:
Still can't you see? In another year's time
you'll be all knocked to bits!
Go somewhere else to find your meals,
else you'll land one that'll be the end of you!
But in one ear and out the other! Look!
Lowering a bucket into the well
at the end of that rope that must weigh a ton,
she nearly went down with the rope into the well!
Hey, you there!
Hey, you there!

윗뜸 우열네 집

봉태네 뒷집
고우열이네 집
그 집 돼지우리는
온 조선 다 돌아보아야
그렇게 깨끗한 돼지우리 없게 깨끗하다
돼지가 아니라
사람에게
밥 흘려도 그냥 주워먹게 깨끗하다
귀한 조상 제사 지내게 깨끗하다
고우열이 아버지야
초생달같이 부지런하여
집 안팎 풀 자라는 데 없고
거미줄 하나 없다
게다가 우열이 어머니
부엌살림 밭살림 정갈하여
첫가을 바깥 추워
집안에 파리 꾀일 때도
파리 두어 마리밖에는
들어올 생각 못 내고 만다
그 집 수챗구멍이
어디 수채인가 산중 개울이지
다른 집은 다 검불깨나 날려도
그 집 마당에는

Wooyol's family house

The house at the back of Pongtae's
belongs to Ko Wooyol.
And that house's pigsty!
Why! you might go all over Korea
and not find one as clean as that,
so clean that if you dropped some food there,
not for pigs but for people,
they would eat it straight off the floor;
clean enough to make offerings
for honored ancestors in.
Ko Wooyol's father?
Diligent as a new moon,
not a single weed growing anywhere about,
not a single cobweb.
What's more, Wooyol's mother
keeps everything so tidy indoors and out
that when the flies come swarming inside
with the first winter frosts,
you'll never find more than a couple there.
And as for that house's drainage outlet!
Well! is that a drain, or a mountain stream?
When spreading millet to dry, in other houses
they spread it out all mixed with leaves and dust,

조 널면 조 멍석에 하늘 받는다
우열이도
우열이 여동생도
몽당빗자루 손에 잡고
식전 일 뚝딱 마친다
헌데
그 집에는 누가 보리 꾸러
쌀 꾸러 가지 않는다
뒤안 석류 익어 적막한데

but in that house's yard a good straw mat
welcomes the sky's visitation.
And Wooyol
with his younger sister
each seizing an old broom, they
clean everything spick-and-span before breakfast.
But
no one ever goes to that house
to borrow a handful of barley or rice.
And round at the back a pomegranate ripens
lonesome.

아베 교장

아베 쓰도무 교장
뚱그런 안경에 고초당초같이 매서운 사람입니다
구두 껍데기 오려낸
슬리퍼 딱딱 소리내어 복도를 걸어오면
각 교실마다 쥐죽어버리는 사람입니다
2학년 때 수신시간에
장차 너희들 뭐가 될래 물었습니다
아이들은
대일본제국 육군대장이 되겠습니다
해군대장이 되겠습니다
야마모또 이소로꾸 각하가 되겠습니다
간호부가 되겠습니다
비행기공장 직공이 되어
비행기 만들어
미영귀축을 이기겠습니다 할 때
아베 교장 나더러 대답해보라 했습니다
나는 벌떡 일어나서
천황폐하가 되겠습니다
그 말이 떨어지자마자
청천벽력이 떨어졌습니다
너는 만세일계 천황폐하를
황공하옵게도 모독했다 네놈은 당장 퇴학이다
이 말에 나는 주저앉아 버렸습니다

Headmaster Abe

Headmaster Abe Sudomu, from Japan:
a fearsome man, with his round glasses,
fiery-hot like hottest pimentos.
When he came walking clip-clop down the hallway
with the clacking sound of his slippers
cut out of a pair of old boots,
he cast a deathly hush over every class.
In my second year during ethics class
he asked us what we hoped to become in the future.
Kids replied:
I want to be a general in the Imperial Army!
I want to become an admiral!
I want to become another Yamamoto Isoroko!
I want to become a nursing orderly!
I want to become a mechanic in a plane factory
          and make planes
to defeat the American and British devils!
Then Headmaster Abe asked me to reply.
I leaped to my feet:
I want to become the Emperor!
Those words were no sooner spoken
than a thunderbolt fell from the blue above:
You have formally blasphemed the venerable name

그러나 담임선생이 빌고
아버지가 새 옷 갈아입고 가서 빌고 빌어서
간신히 퇴학은 면한 대신
몇달 동안 학교 실습지 썩은 보릿단 헤쳐
쓸 만한 보리 가려내는 벌을 받았습니다
날마다 나는 썩은 냄새 속에 갇혀 있었습니다
땡볕 아래서나 빗속에서나 나는 거기서
이 세상에서 내가 혼자임을 깨달았습니다
그 석 달 벌 마친 뒤 수신시간에
아베 교장은 이긴다 이긴다 이긴다고 말했습니다
대일본제국이 이겨
장차 너희들 반도인은 만주와 중국 가서
높고 높은 벼슬 한다고 말했습니다
B-29가 나타났습니다. 그 은빛 4발비행기가 왔습니다
교장은 큰소리로 말했습니다
저것이 귀축이다 저것이 적이라고 겁도 없이 말했습니다
그러나 아베 교장의 어깨에는 힘이 없었습니다
큰소리가 적어지며 끝내는 혼자의 넋두리였습니다
그 뒤 8·15가 왔습니다. 그는 울며 떠났습니다

of his Imperial Majesty: you are expelled this instant!
On hearing that, I collapsed into my seat.
But the form-master pleaded,
my father put on clean clothes and came and pleaded,
and by the skin of my teeth, instead of expulsion,
I was punished by being sent to spend a few months
sorting through a stack of rotten barley
that stood in the school grounds,
separating out the still useable grains.
I was imprisoned every day in a stench of decay
and there, under scorching sun and in beating rain,
I realized I was all alone in the world.
Soon after those three months of punishment were over,
during ethics class Headmaster Abe said:
We're winning, we're winning, we're winning!
Once the great Japanese army has won the war, in the future
you peninsula people will go to Manchuria, go to China,
and take important positions in government offices!
That's what he said.
        Then a B-29 appeared,
and as the silver 4-engined plane passed overhead
our Headmaster cried out in a big voice:
They're devils! That's the enemy! he cried fearlessly.

But his shoulders drooped.
His shout died away into a solitary mutter.
August 15 came. Liberation.
He left for Japan in tears.

Runny

Nobody's around, they're all out working.
A small kid left on his own squats
beneath the eaves, playing with a worm.
After that, once the worm's gone,
he digs up some earth to gnaw,
and plays, just plays.
The whole village is empty.
One plump hen
is there on its own too.
The kid's on his own too.
He's not been put on the family register yet,
not even been given a name but
he often has the runs so he's called Runny, Runny.
After playing there alone
he falls asleep on the bare ground
then the shade moves away, so he wakes up
and cries a bit.
Nobody knows he's crying
but
that's not loneliness, it's belief.
Belief he'll grow up okay though left on his own.
Belief he's at one with this world
though he plays on his own.

물캐똥이

다 일 나가고 없다
어린것 혼자
처마 밑에서 지렁이 건드리며 논다
그러다가
지렁이 가면
흙 파먹으며 논다 잘 논다
마을 전체가 텅 비었다
씨암탉이나 한 마리
그놈도 혼자 있고
어린것도 혼자 있다
아직 호적에도 안 올린 놈
이름도 없는 놈
물캐똥 잘 싸니 물캐똥아 물캐똥아라 부른다
혼자 놀다가 맨 땅에서 자고
그늘 벗겨져 깨고 나서
한번 울어 본다
아무도 운 줄 모른다
그러나
이것이 외로움이 아니라 믿음이다
혼자 두어도 잘 자라는 믿음이다
혼자 놀아도
이 세상과 함께 있는 믿음이다
그러지 않고서야

How else would they dare?
Poor little Runny!
How else would they dare?
How else would they dare?

어린것 물캐똥아
그러지 않고서야
그러지 않고서야

Lee Chongnam

When children cry, if you tell them:
A roaring tiger will come,
a big tiger will come
and carry you off if you cry!
the crying goes on;
but if you say:
They'll take you to Sinpung-ri police box!
then the crying stops as if by magic.
And grown-ups too,
when they pass before Sinpung-ri police box
with the three trays of eggs they're selling,
they feel as if they've stolen them somewhere, and
their hearts beat two or three times faster than normal.
One fellow who simply took to his heels
as he went by was called in: Hey, you!
by a Japanese cop, and had a hard time.
I had a fright going by there once, too,
as I was following uncle Hongsik
on the way to sell dried pine branches down at the wood store.
A man was coming out with a messed-up face,
his hands tied behind his back.
He was being transferred to Kunsan central police station.
Someone was marching along behind him, holding the rope.

이종남

아이들 울 때 어흥 호랑이 나온다 하면
호랑이가 너 울면 업어간다 하면
울음 그치지 않는데
신풍리 주재소로 잡아간다 하면
무당 만수받이로 울음 딱 그친다
어른들도 신풍리 주재소 앞 지나갈 때는
팔러 가는 달걀 석 줄이
꼭 훔쳐가는 것같이
가슴에 두근반 세근반 방망이질한다
어떤 사람은 주재소 앞 걸음아 나 살려라
달음박질치다가
어이 잠깐 하는 왜놈 순사에게 불려가 혼나기도 했다
홍식이 작은아버지
마른 솔가지 나뭇짐 팔러 가는 길 따라가다가
나도 주재소 앞에서 겁이 났다
누군가가 살피틈 찢어진 얼굴에
등뒤로 두 손 묶여 나오고 있다
군산 본서로 넘겨져 가고 있다
그 사람 뒤에 포승줄 잡고 가는 사람이 있다
그 사람이 누군고 하니
주재소 끄나풀이다
바로 우리 당고모 시동생 이종남이다
그 고약한 사람

And who was that? The police box cat's paw, that's who,
Lee Chongnam, brother-in-law to our grandfather's niece.
That wicked man!
He kicked his wife in the stomach and made her abort.
He turned on his own father and pulled his beard.
But where the Japs were concerned, he was down on his knees,
on his knees and crawling, he was so crazy about them!
At Liberation he should have been first to get it,
but he hid for a while, and when he came out
he was put in charge of Sinpung-ri police box.
He dressed himself up in a policeman's cap and uniform,
and put on airs riding around the district on a bicycle:
tring-a-ling, tring-a-ling, Out of my way!

제 마누라 배 차서
아기 지워버리게 한 사람
제 아버지한테도 대들어 수염 웅켜쥔 사람
한데 왜놈한테는 통 사족을 못써 엎어진다
엎어져 긴다
해방 뒤 그 사람 먼저 벌받아야 하는데
그 사람 숨었다 나와
신풍리 지서 순사 되어
경찰 정모 정복 입고
신풍리 나운리 독점고개 미룡리 자전거 타고
찌르릉 찌르릉 길을 비켜라 하고 으시대었다

Firefly

Summertime firefly, you're a simpleton;
you go dashing through life like an arrow, then die.
And you're the female simpleton that takes him
and has his kids.
Young Suntae and Chaehwan's little girl
used to catch fireflies
and put them inside a gourd flower as a lantern
then with that feeble light
they used to play at husbands and wives
and nighttime housekeeping.
Time passed
and Chaehwan's daughter married a Kunsan stationer
while Suntae remained an old bachelor, and went
to prison for assaulting someone when he was drunk.
Childhood things all left behind,
one of them became just an ordinary housewife
and gave birth to a few babies,
the other was taken into custody, judged,
and put on prison garb.
But one day another old bachelor
got put in the same prison cell.
Lo and behold, he came from the house
next door to the Kunsan stationer's store.

개똥벌레

여름날 개똥벌레
너는 쏜살같이 달려가 죽는 숫놈이거라
너는 그 숫놈 받아 새끼 치는 암놈이거라
순태하고
중뜸 재환이 딸하고
개똥벌레 잡아
호박꽃 초롱에 담아
그 멍든 불빛 비치며
서방 각시 놀이 하였지
밤 소꿉놀이 하였지
세월이 흘러
재환네 딸은 군산 문방구집으로 시집가고
순태는 늙다리 총각으로
술 먹고 사람 패어 형무소 갔다
어린시절 다 가버리고
한 사람은 아무개 마누라 되어
새끼 서넛 퍼질러 낳고
한 사람은 용수 쓰고 재판받아 붉은 옷 입었지
그런데 형무소 한방에
한 떠꺼머리 사내가 들어왔지
알고 보니 명치정 문방구 옆집 사내였지
얘기 얘기 하다가
문방구집 마누라 얘기가 나왔지

312

Talking and talking,
at last the talk turned to the housewife there.
Her husband, he said, had given her four kids
and yet he'd been with the bargirl too
and made her a baby as well,
and every time he came home drunk
he would knock his wife all over the floor;
at which Suntae's eyes filled with tears.
God forbid! As soon as I get out of here
I'll tear off his prick, and his balls as well!
But after a year in prison the firmest resolves
all just vanish into thin air, you know.
Nightingales sing, then fly away.

그 집 사내
새끼 넷 낳고도
술집 계집 붙어
거기서 새끼 낳고
술 취하면 본마누라 엎어치고 메어치기 일쑤라고
순태의 눈에 눈물이 그렁
어디 봐라 내가 나가던 머리로
네놈 좆 뽑고 불알 발라버릴테다
그러나 감옥살이 1년 넘으면
굳은 결심 다 풀려버리지
소쩍새 울다 떠나버리지

『한국문학 영역총서』를 펴내며

한국문학을 본격적으로 번역하여 해외에 소개하는 일이 필요함을 우리는 오래 전부터 절실히 느껴 왔다. 그러나 좋은 번역을 만나기는 좋은 창작품을 만나는 것 못지 않게 어렵다. 운이 좋아서 좋은 번역이 있을 경우에는 또한 출판의 기회를 얻기가 쉽지 않다. 서구의 유수한 출판사들은 시장성을 앞세워 지명도가 높지 않은 한국의 문학작품을 출판하기를 꺼린다. 한국 문학의 지명도가 높아지려면 먼저 훌륭하게 번역된 작품들이 세계적인 명성이 있는 출판사에서 출판이 되어 널리 보급이 되어야 하는데, 설혹 훌륭한 번역이 있다 하더라도 이 작품들이 해외에서 출판될 기회가 극히 제한되어 있어서, 지명도를 높일 길이 막막해지는 악순환을 거듭하는 것이 현실이다. 이런 현실을 타개하는 길은 좋은 작품을 제대로 번역하여 우리 손으로 책답게 출판하여 세계의 독자들에게 내놓는 데서 찾을 수밖에 없다. 이런 일을 하기 위해 도서출판 답게에서 "한국 문학 영역총서"를 세상에 내놓는다.

「답게」영역총서는 한영 대역판으로 출판되며, 이 총서는 광범위한 독자층을 위하여 만들어진 것이다. 무엇보다도 이 총서를 통해 해외의 많은 문학 독자들이 한국 문학을 알게 되기를 희망한다. 이 총서는 또한 국내외에서 한국학을 공부하거나 영어로 번역된 한국 작품을 필요로 하는 영어 사용권의 모든 사람들과 한국 문학의 전문적인 번역자들을 위한 것이기도 하다. 전문 번역인들은 동료 번역자들의 작업을 자신들의 것과 비교함으로써 보다 나은 새로운 번역 방법을 모색할 수 있을 것이다. 고급한 영어를 배우기를 원하는 한국의 독자들도 대역판으로 출간되는 이 총서를 읽음으로써, 언어가 어떻게 문학적으로 신비롭게 또 절묘하게 쓰이는지를 깨닫는 등 많은 것을 얻을 수 있을 것이다.

아무리 말쑥하게 잘 만들어진 책이라도 그 내용이 신통치 않으면 결코 책다운 책일 수 없다는 자명한 이유에서, 「답게」 영역총서는 좋은 작품을 골라 최선의 질로 번역한 책만을 출판할 것이다. 또한 새로운 번역자의 발굴과 격려가 이 총서 발간의 목적 가운데 하나이다. 답게 출판사가 발행하는 이 총서가 한국 문학의 번역의 중요성을 다시 한번 일깨우고, 문학 작품의 번역이라는 불가능한 꿈을 가능하게 하려는 번역자들의 노력에 보탬이 되기를 바란다. 이런 시도가 여러 가지로 유용하고 또 도전적인 것이 될 때, 더 나아가서는 잘 번역된 한국 작품의 전세계적인 출판 작업이 이루어지는 단초를 마련할 수 있을 때, 이 선구적인 계획은 진정으로 성공적인 것이 될 것이다.

김 영 무 (서울대 영문과 교수)

Series Editor's Afterword

Extensive translation of Korean literature for the foreign readers has for many years been felt a pressing need. But to fall·upon a good translation is much harder than to discern a good original work. If we are fortunate enough to secure a good translation, it is often very difficult to get it published abroad.

The major publishers of the western world are not yet prepared to run the risk of publishing works of relatively unknown Korean literature. Yet if Korean literature is to achieve worldwide fame, it first of all needs to be well translated, and then put into circulation throughout the world by those very publishers which are so reluctant to publish even good translations of Korean literature. It is a vicious circle: no publication without fame but no fame without publication. To save the situation, we should perhaps try to make available to readers abroad choice translations we ourselves have published in editions of high quality. The DapGae English Translations of Korean Literature series has been launched with this aim.

Each volume of the DapGae series will be a bilingual edition. We expect a wide-ranging audience for the series. It is our primary hope that it will help introduce many foreign readers to the world of Korean literature. The series is especially intended to serve English-speaking students enrolled in Korean studies programs and all who need translations of Korean literature, as well as those who may wish to compare their own translations with the translations of fellow translators in order to find new and better ways of translating. Korean readers studying advanced English can also benefit from reading these bilingual editions: the experience may help them to recognize the mystery of true mastery of the literary use of language.

However well designed a book may be, it cannot properly serve its purpose if the contents are mediocre. For that reason, the DapGae series will strive to introduce to the readers of the world the best translations of the finest works of Korean literature. One of the objectives of the series is to find and encourage new talents in English translation. We hope that the DapGae English Translations of Korean Literature series will serve in some small way to refocus attention upon the importance of translating Korean literature into good English and to make possible the impossible dream of literary translation. This pioneering project will be a true success not only if it proves useful and challenging but also if it paves the way for the publication of fine translations of Korean literature on a worldwide scale.

Young-Moo Kim
Department of English
Seoul National University